Splunk Essentials

Second Edition

A fast-paced and practical guide to demystifying big data and transforming it into operational intelligence

Betsy Page Sigman
Erickson Delgado

BIRMINGHAM - MUMBAI

Splunk Essentials

Second Edition

First published: February 2015

Second Edition: September 2016

Production reference: 1260916

Published by Packt Publishing Ltd.

Livery Place

35 Livery Street

Birmingham B3 2PB, UK.

ISBN 978-1-78588-946-2

www.packtpub.com

Credits

Authors

Betsy Page Sigman
Erickson Delgado

Reviewer

Somesh Soni

Commissioning Editor

Veena Pagare

Acquisition Editor

Vinay Argekar

Content Development Editor

Nikhil Borkar

Technical Editor

Madhunikita Sunil Chindarkar

Copy Editor

Safis Editing

Project Coordinator

Suzanne Coutinho

Proofreader

Safis Editing

Indexer

Rekha Nair

Production Coordinator

Aparna Bhagat

About the Authors

Betsy Page Sigman is a distinguished professor at the McDonough School of Business at Georgetown University in Washington, D.C. She has taught courses in statistics, project management, databases, and electronic commerce for the last 17 years and has been recognized with awards for teaching and service. Before arriving at Georgetown, she worked at George Mason University, the U.S. Bureau of the Census, Decision/Making/Information, the American Enterprise Institute, and the Social Science Data Center (now Roper Center) at the University of Connecticut.

Her recent publications include a Harvard Business case study and a Harvard Business review article, articles in the Decision Sciences Journal of Innovative Education and Decision Line, and a case study in Educause Review Online. Additionally, she is a frequent media commentator on technological issues and big data.

A big thank you to Nikhil Borkar and Vinay Argekar and the other editors and staff at Packt Publishing for your help in every step along the way to finishing this book. Thanks also to my colleagues and students at the McDonough School of Business at Georgetown University. Thanks especially to Bill Garr, Rob Pongsajapan, Marie Selvanandin, and Kristin Bolling, and the Center for New Designs in Learning and Scholarship (CNDLS), for exploring the exciting world of big data and Splunk together. It has been a wonderful place to learn, grow, and serve for the last 16 years.

I need to thank my brothers, Tim and Rick Page, for being there to challenge and encourage me throughout my life. Most of all, I want to thank my brilliant and wonderful husband, Chuck, my astonishing daughter and son-in-law, Page and Daniel Thies, and my three sons. Johnny, thanks for always inspiring me technologically; Richard, thanks for your sense of humor that keeps us all laughing; and James, thanks for always being there for all of us. Edward and Peter, the grandsons who light up all our lives, are too young to read this now. They were born into an extraordinary world—one that I hope and pray technology will continue to improve.

Erickson Delgado is an enterprise architect who loves to mine and analyze data. He began using Splunk in version 4.0 and has pioneered the use of the application in his current work. In the earlier parts of his career, he worked with start-up companies in the Philippines to help build their open source infrastructure. He then worked in the cruise industry as a shipboard IT manager, and he loved it. From there, he was recruited to work at the company's headquarters as a software engineer.

He has developed applications with Python and Node.js. He is interested in Go and is rediscovering programming with C/C++. He is crazy about visualization platforms and tools. In recent years, he has engaged himself with employing DevOps in his work.

Since Erickson's routine revolves around technical practices, he blows off steam by saltwater fishing, mountain biking, crafting robots, and touring the country. He lives in Orlando.

To my wife, Emma, thank you for the never-ending support and patience.

About the Reviewer

Somesh Soni is a Splunk consultant with over 11 years of IT experience. He has a bachelor's degree (Hons.) in computer science and has been interested in exploring and learning new technologies throughout his life. He has extensive experience in consulting, architecture, administration, and development in Splunk. He's proficient in various programming languages and tools, including C#.NET/VB.NET, SSIS, and SQL Server.

Somesh is currently working as a Splunk Master with Randstad Technologies. His activities are focused on consulting, implementation, admin, architecture, and support-related activities for Splunk. He started his career with the one of the top three Indian IT giants. He has executed projects for major Fortune 500 companies such as Coca Cola, Wells Fargo, Microsoft, and Capital Group. He has performed in various capacities, including Technical Architect, Technical Lead, Onsite Coordinator, and Technology Analyst.

Somesh has been a great contributor to the Splunk community and has consistently been at the top of the list. He is a member of Splunk Trust 2015-16 and overall one of the topmost contributors to the Splunk Answers community.

I would like to thank my family and colleagues, who have always encouraged and supported me to follow my dreams, and my friends, who put up with all my crazy antics while I went on a Splunk exploratory journey and listened with patience to all the tips and tricks of Splunk that I shared with them.

Last but not least, I would like to express my gratitude to the entire team at Packt Publishing for giving me this opportunity.

www.PacktPub.com

For support files and downloads related to your book, please visit www.PacktPub.com.

Did you know that Packt offers eBook versions of every book published, with PDF and ePub files available? You can upgrade to the eBook version at www.PacktPub.com and as a print book customer, you are entitled to a discount on the eBook copy. Get in touch with us at service@packtpub.com for more details.

At www.PacktPub.com, you can also read a collection of free technical articles, sign up for a range of free newsletters and receive exclusive discounts and offers on Packt books and eBooks.

https://www.packtpub.com/mapt

Get the most in-demand software skills with Mapt. Mapt gives you full access to all Packt books and video courses, as well as industry-leading tools to help you plan your personal development and advance your career.

Why subscribe?

- Fully searchable across every book published by Packt
- Copy and paste, print, and bookmark content
- On demand and accessible via a web browser

Table of Contents

Preface

In *Splunk Essentials, Second Edition*, we have added many more features that readers should find useful. Splunk Enterprise Software, or Splunk, is an extremely powerful tool for searching, exploring, and visualizing data of all types. Splunk is becoming increasingly popular, as more and more businesses, both large and small, discover its ease and usefulness. Analysts, managers, students, and others can quickly learn how to use the data from their systems, networks, web traffic, and social media to make attractive and informative reports. This is a straightforward, practical, and quick introduction to Splunk that should have you making reports and gaining insights from your data in no time. We have added a number of helpful hints and exercises that will help you get up to speed with Splunk in no time. Throughout the book, we have provided step-by-step instructions, pointers, and illustrations to help you on your way.

What this book covers

Chapter 1, *Splunk in Action*, introduces you to Splunk Enterprise Software and its powerful capabilities.

Chapter 2, *Bringing in Data*, explains indexing and searching in Splunk, and introduces other data concepts that are important to understand.

Chapter 3, *Search Processing Language*, develops your skills in using Search Processing Language (SPL).

Chapter 4, *Data Models and Pivot*, shows you how to create a data model as well as a pivot table using Splunk.

Chapter 5, *Data Optimization, Reports, Alerts, and Accelerating Searches*, explores how to use data optimization and search acceleration with Splunk, and how to create effective reports and alerts.

Chapter 6, *Panes of Glass*, takes you step-by-step through the development of dashboard.

Chapter 7, *Splunk SDK for JavaScript and D3.js*, instructs you on how to use a Splunk SDK and D3 to create effective and attractive website visualizations.

Chapter 8, *HTTP Event Collector*, introduces how to use Splunk to monitor HTTP events.

Chapter 9, *Best Practices and Advanced Queries*, overviews various best practices for using Splunk and gives details on advanced queries that can be used to take advantage of Splunk's many rich capabilities.

What you need for this book

Most personal computers today can run Splunk easily. For more technical details see `http://docs.splunk.com/Documentation/6.4/Installation/Chooseyourplatform`.

Who this book is for

Splunk Essentials, Second Edition, is intended for the Splunk developer, software engineer, businessperson, analyst, or student who wants to quickly learn how to use Splunk to manage data. Perhaps you have heard about this technology that is being used quite often now in fields like systems analysis, cyber security, and machine data management. In a matter of hours, this book will help you understand how to bring in data of all types, store it, and use it to create effective reports and dashboards. It would be helpful to have a bit of familiarity with basic computer concepts, but no prior experience is required.

Conventions

In this book, you will find a number of text styles that distinguish between different kinds of information. Here are some examples of these styles and an explanation of their meaning.

Code words in text, database table names, folder names, filenames, file extensions, pathnames, dummy URLs, user input, and Twitter handles are shown as follows: "It is essentially a collection of databases that is, by default, located at `$SPLUNK_HOME/var/lib/splunk`."

A block of code is set as follows:

```
[wineventlogs]
coldPath = $SPLUNK_DB\wineventlogs\colddb
homePath = $SPLUNK_DB\wineventlogs\db
maxTotalDataSizeMB = 100
thawedPath = $SPLUNK_DB\wineventlogs\thaweddb
```

Any command-line input or output is written as in two ways in this book. Be careful when copying commands with quotation marks. It is best to type in the entire search command to avoid problems.

If it is a Windows command, the command will be written as follows:

```
C:\> notepad c:\splunk\etc\apps\destinations\local\indexes.conf
```

If it is a Splunk command, the command will be written as follows:

```
SPL> index=main /booking/confirmation earliest=-24h@h | timechart
      count span=15m
```

New terms and **important words** are shown in bold. Words that you see on the screen, for example, in menus or dialog boxes, appear in the text like this: "Underneath Selected Fields, you will see Interesting Fields."

Warnings or important notes appear in a box like this.

Tips and tricks appear like this.

Reader feedback

Feedback from our readers is always welcome. Let us know what you think about this book-what you liked or disliked. Reader feedback is important for us as it helps us develop titles that you will really get the most out of. To send us general feedback, simply e-mail feedback@packtpub.com, and mention the book's title in the subject of your message. If there is a topic that you have expertise in and you are interested in either writing or contributing to a book, see our author guide at www.packtpub.com/authors.

Customer support

Now that you are the proud owner of a Packt book, we have a number of things to help you to get the most from your purchase.

Downloading the example code

You can download the example code files for this book from your account at `http://www.p acktpub.com`. If you purchased this book elsewhere, you can visit `http://www.packtpub.c om/support` and register to have the files e-mailed directly to you.

You can download the code files by following these steps:

1. Log in or register to our website using your e-mail address and password.
2. Hover the mouse pointer on the **SUPPORT** tab at the top.
3. Click on **Code Downloads & Errata**.
4. Enter the name of the book in the **Search** box.
5. Select the book for which you're looking to download the code files.
6. Choose from the drop-down menu where you purchased this book from.
7. Click on **Code Download**.

Once the file is downloaded, please make sure that you unzip or extract the folder using the latest version of:

- WinRAR / 7-Zip for Windows
- Zipeg / iZip / UnRarX for Mac
- 7-Zip / PeaZip for Linux

The code bundle for the book is also hosted on GitHub at `https://github.com/PacktPubl ishing/Splunk-Essentials-Second-Edition`. We also have other code bundles from our rich catalog of books and videos available at `https://github.com/PacktPublishing/`. Check them out!

Downloading the color images of this book

We also provide you with a PDF file that has color images of the screenshots/diagrams used in this book. The color images will help you better understand the changes in the output. You can download this file from `https://www.packtpub.com/sites/default/files/down loads/SplunkEssentialsSecondEdition_ColorImages.pdf`.

Errata

Although we have taken every care to ensure the accuracy of our content, mistakes do happen. If you find a mistake in one of our books-maybe a mistake in the text or the code-we would be grateful if you could report this to us. By doing so, you can save other readers from frustration and help us improve subsequent versions of this book. If you find any errata, please report them by visiting http://www.packtpub.com/submit-errata, selecting your book, clicking on the **Errata Submission Form** link, and entering the details of your errata. Once your errata are verified, your submission will be accepted and the errata will be uploaded to our website or added to any list of existing errata under the Errata section of that title.

To view the previously submitted errata, go to https://www.packtpub.com/books/content/support and enter the name of the book in the search field. The required information will appear under the **Errata** section.

Piracy

Piracy of copyrighted material on the Internet is an ongoing problem across all media. At Packt, we take the protection of our copyright and licenses very seriously. If you come across any illegal copies of our works in any form on the Internet, please provide us with the location address or website name immediately so that we can pursue a remedy.

Please contact us at copyright@packtpub.com with a link to the suspected pirated material.

We appreciate your help in protecting our authors and our ability to bring you valuable content.

Questions

If you have a problem with any aspect of this book, you can contact us at questions@packtpub.com, and we will do our best to address the problem.

1
Splunk in Action

Splunk, whose name was inspired by the process of exploring caves, or *spelunking*, helps analysts, operators, programmers, and many others explore many types of data, including raw machine data from their organizations, by collecting, analyzing, and acting on them. This multinational company, cofounded by Michael Baum, Rob Das, and Erik Swan, has a core product called Splunk Enterprise. This product manages searches, inserts, deletes, filters, and analyzes big data that is generated by machines, as well as many other types of data.

 Throughout the book, we will be covering the fundamental, barebones concepts of Splunk so you can learn quickly and efficiently. We reserve any deep discussion of concepts to Splunk's online documentation. Where necessary, we provide links to help provide you with the practical skills, and examples, so you can get started quickly. All images and exercise materials used in this book are available at `http://github.com/erickson d/splunk-essentials`. Instructions for Mac OS X can also be found in the GitHub repository mentioned in the preceding link.

With very little time, you can achieve direct results using Splunk, which you can access through a free enterprise trial license. While this license limits you to 500 MB of data ingested per day, it will allow you to quickly get up to speed with Splunk and learn the essentials of this powerful software.

The exercises in this chapter may look challenging at first, but if you follow what we've written closely, we believe you will quickly learn the fundamentals you need to use Splunk effectively. Together, we will make the most of the Trial License and give you a visible result that you can use to create valuable insights for your company (and, if you like, proudly show to your friends and coworkers).

Your Splunk.com account

First you will need to register for a Splunk.com account. This is the account that you will use if you decide to purchase a license later. Go ahead and do this now. From here on, the password you use for your Splunk.com account will be referred to as your Splunk.com password.

Obtaining a Splunk.com account

To obtain your Splunk.com account, perform the following steps:

1. Go to the Splunk signup page at `http://www.splunk.com`.
2. In the upper right hand corner, click on **My Account** | **Sign Up**.
3. Enter the information requested.
4. Create a username and password.

You will then need to download the Splunk Enterprise software. Go to `http://download.splunk.com` and select the Splunk Enterprise free download. Choose your operating system, being careful to select 32- or 64-bit (whichever is appropriate in your case; most should select 64-bit, which most computers today use). For Windows, download the `*.msi` file. For Mac OS X, download the `*.dmg` file. In this book, we will work with Version 6.4.1 or later.

The installation is very straightforward. Follow the steps for your particular operating system, whether it be Windows or Mac OS X.

 Make sure that there is no previous installation of Splunk in your system. If there is, uninstall the old version before proceeding with the next steps.

Installing Splunk on Windows

These are the instructions you need to follow to install Splunk on your Windows desktop. Take your time and do not rush the installation. Many chapters in this book will rely on these steps:

1. Run the installer that you downloaded.
2. Check the box to accept the License Agreement and then click on **Customize Options** as shown in the following screenshot:

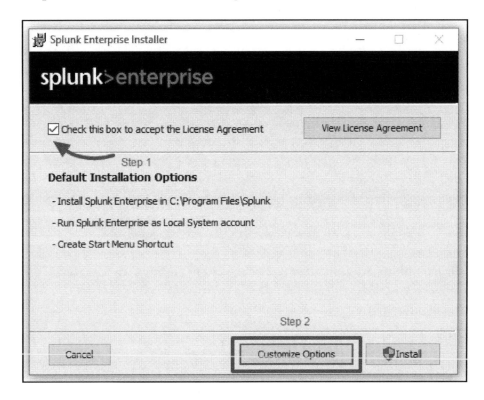

3. Change the **installation path** to C:\Splunk. You will thank us later as it simplifies issuing **Splunk CLI** (**command-line interface**) commands. This is also a best practice used by modern Windows administrators. Remember to eliminate white spaces in directory names as well, as it causes complications with scripting. Click on **Next** to continue as seen in the following screenshot:

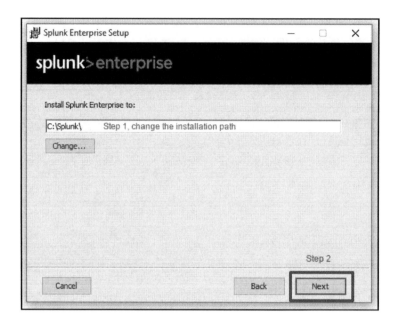

4. Install Splunk Enterprise as the **Local System** and then click on **Next**.
5. Leave the checkbox selected to **Create Start Menu Shortcut**.
6. Click on **Install**.
7. Wait for the installation to complete.
8. Click on **Finish** to complete the installation. It will attempt to launch Splunk for the first time in your default browser.

Throughout the book, you will see references to $SPLUNK_HOME. This will be the installation directory of Splunk. In Windows, as a convention used in this book, $SPLUNK_HOME will be at C:\Splunk.

Logging in the first time

Launch the application the first time in your default browser. You can also manually access the Splunk web page via the `http://localhost:8000` URL.

 Splunk requires you to use a modern browser. It supports most versions of Google Chrome, Firefox, and newer versions of Internet Explorer. It may not support older versions of Internet Explorer.

Log in with the default username and password (**admin : changeme**) as indicated in the following screenshot:

The next step is to change the default administrator password, while keeping the default username. Do not skip this step. Make security an integral part of your day-to-day routine. Choose a password that will be secure:

Assuming all goes well, you will now see the default Splunk **Search & Reporting** dashboard:

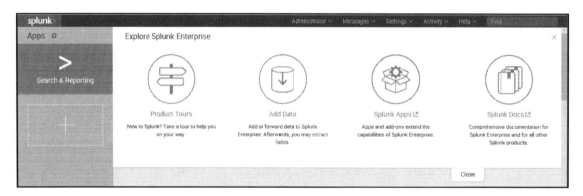

Run a simple search

You are finally ready to run your very first Splunk search query:

1. Go ahead and create your first Splunk search query. Click on the **Search & Reporting** app. You will be introduced to Splunk's very own internal index: this is Splunk's way of *splunking* itself (or collecting detailed information on all its underlying processes).

2. In the **New Search** input, type in the following search query (more about the **Search Processing Language** (**SPL**) in, Chapter 3, *Search Processing Language*):

   ```
   SPL> index=_internal sourcetype=splunkd
   ```

   The SPL> prefix will be used as a convention in this book to indicate a Search command as opposed to the C:\> prefix which indicates a Windows command.

   The underscore before the index name _internal means that it is a system index internally used by Splunk. Omitting the underscore will not yield any result, as internal is not a default index.

3. This search query will have as an output the raw events from the metrics.log file that is stored in the _internal index. A log file keeps track of every event that takes place in the system. The _internal index keeps track of every event that occurs and makes it easily accessible.

4. Take a look at these raw events, as shown in the following screenshot. You will see fields listed on the left side of the screen. The important **Selected Fields** are **host**, **source**, and **sourcetype**. We will go into more detail about these later, but suffice it to say that you will frequently search on one of these, as we have done here. As you can see from the highlighted fields, we indicated that we were looking for events where `sourcetype=splunkd`. Underneath **Selected Fields**, you will see **Interesting Fields**. As you can tell, the purposes of many of these fields are easy to guess:

Creating a Splunk app

It is good practice to create a custom Splunk app to isolate all the changes you make in Splunk. You may never have created an app before, but you will quickly see it is not very difficult. Here we will create a basic app called **Destinations** that we will use throughout this book:

1. Let's access the **Manage Apps** page. There are two ways to do this; you may either click on the **Apps** icon at the *home page* as shown in the following screenshot:

2. Or select **Manage Apps** from the app dropdown in the top navigation bar of the **Search & Reporting** app:

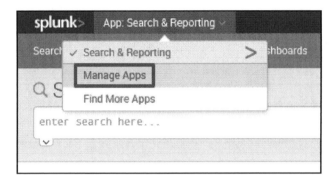

3. At the **Manage Apps** page, click on the **Create app** icon as shown in the following screenshot:

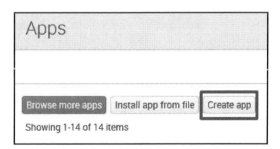

4. Finally, populate the forms with the following information to complete the app creation. When you are done, click on the **Save** button to create your first Splunk app:

5. You have just created your very first Splunk app. Notice that it now appears in the list of apps and it has a status of **Enabled**, meaning it is ready to be used:

Name ⇕	Folder name ⇕	Version ⇕	Update checking ⇕	Visible ⇕	Sharing ⇕	Status ⇕
SplunkForwarder	SplunkForwarder		Yes	No	App | Permissions	Disabled | Enable
SplunkLightForwarder	SplunkLightForwarder		Yes	No	App | Permissions	Disabled | Enable
Webhook Alert Action	alert_webhook	6.3.0	Yes	No	App | Permissions	Enabled | Disable
Apps Browser	appsbrowser	6.3.0	Yes	Yes	App | Permissions	Enabled
Destinations	destinations	None	Yes	Yes	Global | Permissions	Enabled | Disable
framework	framework		Yes	No	App | Permissions	Enabled | Disable
Getting started	gettingstarted	1.0	Yes	Yes	App | Permissions	Disabled | Enable

We will use this bare bones app to complete the exercises in this book, but first we need to make a few important changes:

1. Click the **Permissions** link as show in the preceding screenshot.
2. In the next window, under the **Sharing for config file-only objects** section, select **All apps**.

These steps will ensure that the application will be accessible to the Eventgen add-on that will be installed later in the chapter. Use the following screenshot as a guide:

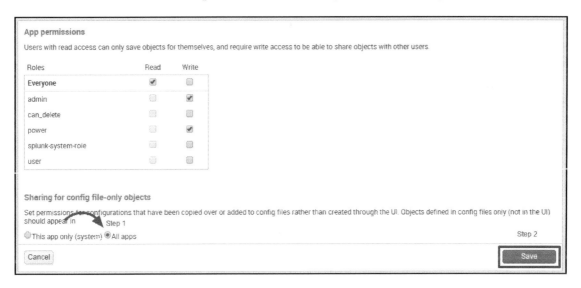

Splunk permissions are always composed of three columns: **Roles**, **Read**, and **Write**. A role refers to certain authorizations or permissions that can be taken on by a user. Selecting **Read** for a particular role grants the set of users in the role permission to view the object. Selecting **Write** will allow the set of users to modify the object. In the preceding screenshot, everyone (all users) will have access to view the Destinations app, but only the admin (you) and a power user can modify it.

Populating data with Eventgen

Machine data is the information produced by the many functions carried out by computers and other mechanical machines. If you work in an environment that is rich in machine data, you will most likely have many sources of readily-available machine inputs for Splunk. However, to facilitate learning in this book, we will use a Splunk add-on called the **Splunk Eventgen** to easily build real-time and randomized web log data. This is the type of data that would be produced by a web-based e-commerce company.

 If you need more detailed information about Eventgen, you can follow the project's GitHub repository at `https://github.com/splunk/eventgen/`.

Here's an important tip. Make it a habit to always launch your command prompt in Administrator mode. This allows you to use commands that are unhindered by Windows security:

1. Right-click on the Windows Start menu icon and select **Search**. In Windows 7, you can click on the Windows icon and the search window will be directly above it. In Windows 10, there is a search bar named **Cortana** next to the Windows icon that you can type into. They both have the same underlying function.

2. In the search bar, type `cmd`.

3. In the search results, look for `command.exe` (Windows 7) or a command prompt (Windows 10), right-click on it, then select **Run as administrator**.

 Familiarize yourself with this step. Throughout the rest of the book, you will be frequently asked to open a command prompt in Administrator mode. You will know if you are in Administrator mode, as it will say Administrator: Command Prompt in the title of the command prompt window.

Installing an add-on

A Splunk add-on extends and enhances the base functionality of Splunk. They also typically enrich data from source for easier analysis. In this section, you will be installing your first add-on called **Splunk Eventgen** that will help us pre-populate Splunk with real-time simulated web data:

1. First we need to install the Eventgen add-on. If you have Git (https://git-scm.com) installed on your machine, you may clone the entire project onto your machine with the following command:

   ```
   C:\> git clone https://github.com/splunk/eventgen.git
   ```

2. You may also download the ZIP file from the Eventgen's public repository, http://github.com/splunk/eventgen, and extract it onto your machine. The download ZIP button is in the lower-right corner of the GitHub repository page.

3. After extracting the ZIP file, copy the entire eventgen directory into the $SPLUNK_HOME/etc/apps/ folder. You may need to rename it from eventgen-master to SA-EventGen if you manually downloaded the ZIP file. The trailing slashes are important. Now open an administrator command prompt and execute the following command:

   ```
   C:\> xcopy eventgen c:\Splunk\etc\apps\SA-Eventgen /O /X /E /H /K
   ```

   In the prompt, type D. Verify the contents of the folder using the following command:

   ```
   C:\> dir c:\Splunk\etc\apps\SA-Eventgen
   ```

These are the contents of the recently-copied `SA-Eventgen` folder as shown in the following screenshot:

```
C:\>dir c:\Splunk\etc\apps\SA-Eventgen
Volume in drive C has no label.
Volume Serial Number is 282F-E3E3

Directory of c:\Splunk\etc\apps\SA-Eventgen

02/04/2016  03:58 AM    <DIR>          .
02/04/2016  03:58 AM    <DIR>          ..
02/04/2016  03:42 AM               162 .gitignore
02/04/2016  03:58 AM    <DIR>          bin
02/04/2016  03:42 AM               677 build.sh
02/04/2016  03:42 AM             1,596 build.xml
02/04/2016  03:58 AM    <DIR>          default
02/04/2016  03:58 AM    <DIR>          lib
02/04/2016  03:42 AM            11,560 LICENSE
02/04/2016  03:58 AM    <DIR>          metadata
02/04/2016  03:58 AM    <DIR>          README
02/04/2016  03:42 AM            11,945 README.md
02/04/2016  03:58 AM    <DIR>          samples
02/04/2016  03:58 AM    <DIR>          tests
               5 File(s)         25,940 bytes
               9 Dir(s)  49,145,090,048 bytes free
```

4. Restart Splunk by selecting the **Settings** dropdown, and under the **SYSTEM** section, click on **Server controls:**

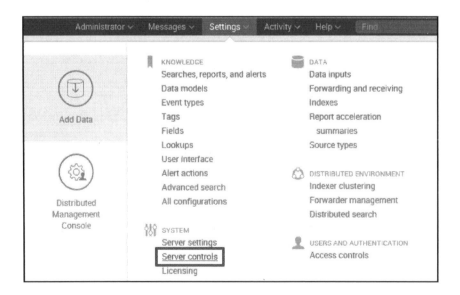

5. On the **Server controls** page, click on the **Restart Splunk** button as shown in the following screenshot. Click **OK** when asked to confirm the restart:

6. The web interface will first notify you that Splunk is restarting in the background, then it will tell you that the restart has been successful. Every time Splunk is restarted, you will be prompted to log in with your credentials. Go ahead and log in.

7. Go to the **Manage Apps** page and confirm that the SA-EventGen application is installed:

You have successfully installed a Splunk add-on.

Controlling Splunk

There are several different ways to stop, start, or restart Splunk. The easiest way is to do it from the web interface, as demonstrated in the preceding section. The web interface, however, only allows you to restart your Splunk instance. It does not offer any other control options.

In Windows, you can also control Splunk through the **Splunkd Service** as shown in the following screenshot. The *d* in the service name, denoting *daemon*, means a background process. Note that the second service, **splunkweb**, is not running. Do not try to start **splunkweb** as it is deprecated and is only there for legacy purposes. The Splunk web application is now bundled in **Splunkd Service:**

Software Protection	Enables the ...		Automatic (D...	Network S...
Splunkd Service	Splunkd is t...	Running	Automatic	Local Syste...
splunkweb (legacy purposes only)	The splunk...		Automatic	Local Syste...
Spot Verifier	Verifies pote...		Manual (Trig...	Local Syste...

The best way to control Splunk is by using the **command-line interface (CLI)**. It may require a little effort to do it, but using the CLI is an essential skill to learn. Remember to always use command prompts in Administrator mode.

In the console or command prompt, type in the following command and hit Enter on your keyboard:

```
C:\> cd \Splunk\bin
```

Here cd is a command that means *change directory*.

While in the C:\Splunk\bin directory, issue the following command to restart Splunk:

```
C:\> C:\Splunk\bin> splunk restart
```

After issuing this command, splunkd will go through its restart process. Here are the other basic parameters that you can pass to the Splunk application to control Splunk:

- splunk status: Tells you if splunkd is running or not
- splunk stop: Stops splunkd and all its processes
- splunk start: Starts splunkd and all its processes
- splunk restart: Restarts splunkd and all its processes

Doing this in the console gives the added benefit of verbose messages. A verbose message is a message with a lot of information in it. Such messages can be useful for making sure the system is working correctly or troubleshooting any errors.

A successful restart of splunkd has the following output (which may vary):

```
Checking kvstore port [8191]: open
Checking configuration...  Done.
Checking critical directories...        Done
Checking indexes...
        Validated: _audit _internal _introspection _thefishbucket history main summary
Done
Checking filesystem compatibility...  Done
Checking conf files for problems...
Done
Checking default conf files for edits...
Validating installed files against hashes from 'C:\Splunk\splunk-6.3.0-aa7d4b1ccb80-windows-64-manifest'
All installed files intact.
Done
All preliminary checks passed.

Starting splunk server daemon (splunkd)...

Splunkd: Starting (pid 3676)
Done
```

Configuring Eventgen

We are almost there. Proceed by first downloading the exercise materials that will be used in this book. Open an Administrator command prompt and make sure you are in the root of the C: drive. If you are using Git, clone the entire project with this Git command:

```
C:\> git clone https://github.com/ericksond/splunk-essentials.git
```

You can alternatively just download the ZIP file and extract it in your computer using https://github.com/ericksond/splunk-essentials/archive/master.zip.

The Eventgen configuration you will need for the exercises in this book has been packaged and is ready to go. We are not going into the details of how to configure Eventgen. If you are interested in learning more about Eventgen, visit the project page at http://github.com/splunk/eventgen.

Follow these instructions to proceed:

1. Extract the project ZIP file into your local machine. Open an administrator console and CD into the directory where you extracted the file.

2. Create a new `samples` directory in the Destinations Splunk app. The path of this new directory will be `$SPLUNK_HOME/etc/apps/destinations/samples`:

   ```
   C:\> mkdir c:\splunk\etc\apps\destinations\samples
   ```

3. Copy all the `*.sample` files from `/labs/chapter01/eventgen` of the extracted project directory into the newly-created `samples` directory. You can also copy and paste using the GUI if you prefer it:

   ```
   C:\> copy splunk-essentials\labs\chapter01\eventgen\*.sample
        c:\Splunk\etc\apps\destinations\samples\
   ```

4. Now copy the `eventgen.conf` into the `$SPLUNK_HOME/etc/apps/destinations/local` directory. You can also copy and paste using the GUI if you prefer it:

   ```
   C:\> copy splunk-essentials\labs\chapter01\eventgen\eventgen.conf
        c:\Splunk\etc\apps\destinations\local\
   ```

5. Grant the `SYSTEM` account full access permissions to the `eventgen.conf` file. This is a very important step. You can either do it using the following `icacls` command or change it using the Windows GUI:

   ```
   C:\> icacls c:\Splunk\etc\apps\destinations\local\eventgen.conf
        /grant SYSTEM:F
   ```

   A successful output of this command will look like this:

   ```
   processed file: c:\Splunk\etc\apps\destinations\local\eventgen.conf
   Successfully processed 1 files; Failed processing 0 files
   ```

6. Restart Splunk.

Viewing the Destinations app

Next we will see our Destinations app in action! Remember that we have configured it to draw events from a prototype web company. That is what we did when we set it up to work with Eventgen. Now let's look at some of our data:

1. After a successful restart, log back in to Splunk and proceed to your new Destinations app:

2. In the **Search** field, type this search query and select Enter:

    SPL> index=main

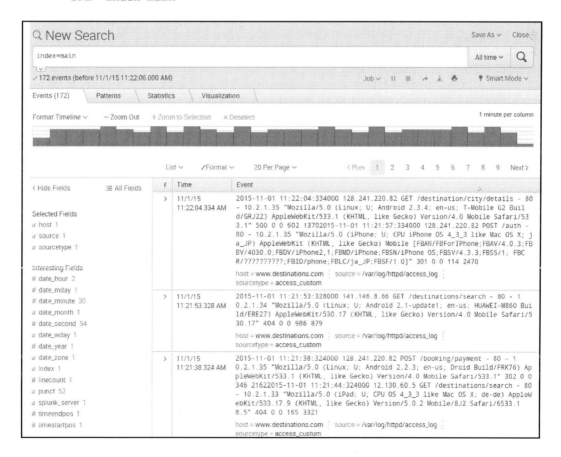

Examine the event data that your new app is enabling to come into Splunk. You will see a lot of references to browsers, systems, and so forth: the kinds of information that make a web-based e-commerce company run.

Try changing the time range to **Real-time (5 minute window)** to see the data flow in before your eyes:

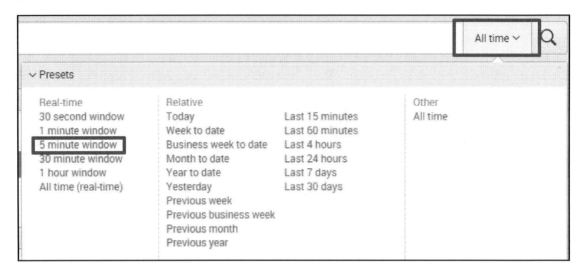

Congratulations! You now have real-time web log data that we can use in subsequent chapters.

Creating your first dashboard

Now that we have data ingested, it is time to use it in order to derive something meaningful out of it. You are still in the Destinations app, correct? We will show you the basic routine when creating new dashboards and dashboard panels.

Copy and paste the following search query in the **Search Field**, then hit *Enter*:

```
SPL> index=main /booking/confirmation earliest=-24h@h | timechart
     count span=15m
```

After the search results render, click on the **Visualization** tab. This will switch your view into visualization so you can readily see how your data will look. By default, it should already be using the **Column Chart** as shown in the following screenshot. If it does not, then use the screenshot as a guide on how to set it:

Now that you can see your **Column Chart**, it is time to save it as a dashboard. Click on **Save As** in the upper-right corner of the page, then select **Dashboard Panel** as shown in the following screenshot:

Now let's fill up that dashboard panel information, as seen in the following screenshot. Make sure to select the **Shared in App** in the **Dashboard Permissions** section:

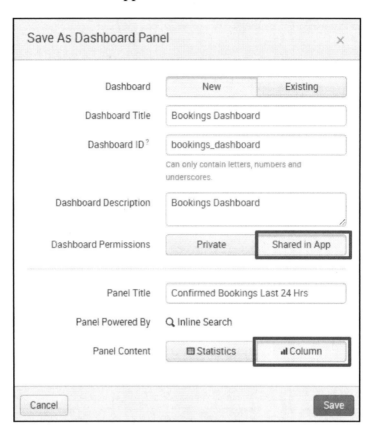

Finish up by clicking **View Dashboard** in the next prompt:

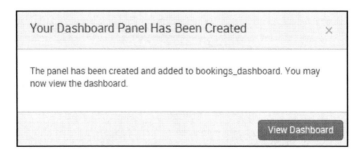

You have created your very first Splunk dashboard with a panel that tells you the number of confirmed bookings in the last 24 hours at 15-minute intervals. Time to show it to your boss!

Take that well-deserved coffee break. You now have a fully-functional Splunk installation with live data. Leave Splunk running for 2 hours or so. After a few hours, you can stop Splunk if you need to rest for a bit to suppress indexing and restart it when you're ready to proceed into the next chapters. Do you recall how to control Splunk from the command line?

```
C:\>   C:\Splunk\bin> splunk stop
       C:\Splunk\bin> splunk start
```

Summary

In this chapter, you learned a number of basic Splunk concepts that you need to get started with this powerful tool. You learned how to install Splunk and configure a new Splunk app. You ran a simple search to ensure that the application is functional. You then installed a Splunk add-on called Eventgen, which you used to populate dummy data into Splunk in real time. You were shown how to control Splunk using the web user interface and the command-line interface. Finally, you created your very first Splunk dashboard. Now we will go on in Chapter 2, *Bringing in Data*, to learn more about how to input data.

2
Bringing in Data

The process of collecting data with Splunk is enhanced, as its system makes it easy to get data from many types of computerized systems, which are responsible for much of the data produced today. Such data is frequently referred to as machine data. And since much of this is streaming data, Splunk is especially useful, as it can handle streaming data quickly and efficiently. Additionally, Splunk can collect data from many other sources.

In this chapter, you will learn about Splunk and its role in big data, as well as the most common methods of ingesting data into Splunk. The chapter will also introduce essential concepts such as forwarders, indexes, events, event types, fields, sources, and source types. It is paramount that you learn this early on as it will empower you to gather more data. In this chapter we will cover the following topics:

- Splunk and big data
- Splunk data sources
- Splunk indexes
- Inputting data into Splunk
- Splunk events and fields

Splunk and big data

Splunk is useful for datasets of all types, and it allows you to use big data tools on datasets of all sizes. But with the recent focus on big data, its usefulness becomes even more apparent. Big data is a term used everywhere these days, but one that few people understand. In this part of the chapter, we will discuss aspects of big data and the terms that describe those aspects.

Streaming data

Much of the data that is large and comes quickly does not need to be kept. For instance, consider a mechanical plant; there can be many sensors that collect data on all parts of the assembly line. The significance of this data is primarily to be able to alert someone to a possible upcoming problem (through noticing a bad trend) or to a current problem (by drawing attention to a metric that has exceeded some designated level); and much of it does not need to be kept for a long period of time. Often this type of data loses its importance once its timeliness expires and its main usefulness may just be in providing a sample measurement that can be used for historical records. Fast-moving data such as this is called streaming data, and Splunk, with its ability to create alerts, allows organizations to use this data to make sure they prevent, or act quickly on, problems that can occur.

Latency of data

The term **latency,** in regards to data, refers to the delay in how speedily it is entered into the system for analysis. Splunk is able to analyze data in real time with no latency issues when deployed on hardware that is sufficient to handle the indexing and searching workload. For example, if an alert goes off, a system can be immediately shut down if there is no latency in the data. If a denial of a service attack (a cyberattack that can dramatically hurt an e-commerce company's bottom line) is taking place, Splunk can be quickly used to figure out what is happening almost immediately.

Sparseness of data

Splunk is also excellent for dealing with sparse data. Much data in retailing environments is considered sparse. Consider a store that has many products but where most people just buy a few of them on any given shopping trip. If the store's database has fields specifying how many items of a particular type have been purchased by each customer, most of the fields would be empty if the time interval under consideration was short. We would say then that the data is sparse. In Splunk, the sparseness of data in a search ranges from dense (meaning that a result is obtained 10 percent of the time or more) to sparse (from 0.01 to 1 percent of the time). This can also extend to super sparse, or, for a better definition, trying to find a needle in a haystack (which is less than 0.01 percent), and even to rare, which is just a handful of cases.

Splunk data sources

Splunk was invented as a way to keep track of and analyze machine data coming from a variety of computerized systems. It is a powerful platform for doing just that. But since its invention, it has been used for a myriad of different data types, including machine data, log data (which is a type of machine data), and social media data. The various types of data that Splunk is often used for are explained in the next few sections.

Machine data

As mentioned previously, much of Splunk's data is machine data. Machine data is data created each time a machine does something, even if it is as seemingly insignificant as a tick on a clock. Each tick has information about its exact time (down to the second) and source, and each of these becomes a field associated with the event (the tick). The term "machine data" can be used in reference to a wide variety of data coming from computerized machines, from servers to operating systems to controllers for robotic assembly arms. Almost all machine data includes the time it was created or when the actual event took place. If no timestamp is included, then Splunk will need to find a date in the source name or filename based on the file's last modification time. As a last resort, it will stamp the event with the time it was indexed into Splunk.

Web logs

Web logs are invaluable sources of information for anyone interested in learning about how their website is used. Deep analysis of web logs can answer questions about which pages are visited most, which pages have problems (people leaving quickly, discarded shopping carts, and other aborted actions), and many others. Google, in early 2014, was registering as many as 20 billion websites each day; you can find more information about this at `http://w ww.roche.com/media/roche_stories/roche-stories-214-1-22.htm`.

Data files

Splunk can read in data from basically all types of files containing clear data, or as they put it, any data. Splunk can also decompress the following types of files: `tar`, `gz`, `bz2`, `tar.gz`, `tgz`, `tbz`, `tbz2`, `zip`, and `z`, along with many others.

Social media data

An enormous amount of data is produced by social media every second. Consider the fact that 1.13 billion people (https://zephoria.com/top-15-valuable-facebook-statistics/) login to Facebook each day and they spend, on average, 20 minutes at a time interacting with the site. Any Facebook (or any other social media) interaction creates a significant amount of data, even those that don't include the more data-intensive acts, such as posting a picture, audio file, or a video. Other social media sources of data include popular sites such as Twitter, LinkedIn, Pinterest, and Google+ in the U.S., and QZone, WeChat, and Weibo in China. As a result of the increasing number of social media sites, the volume of social media data created continues to grow dramatically each year.

Other data types

Almost any type of data works in Splunk. Some of these types include scripted inputs and modular inputs. Sometimes you may want to include a script that sets data up so that it is indexed the way you want. Or you may want to include data coming from a source that is unusual in some way, and you want to make sure that the fields are set up the way they should be. For these reasons, it is nice to know that you can use Python scripts, Windows batch files, shell scripts, and other utilities to make sure your inputs are formatted correctly. You will see the other data types listed when we add data to Splunk shortly.

Creating indexes

Indexes are where Splunk Enterprise stores all the data it has processed. It is essentially a collection of databases that is, by default, located at $SPLUNK_HOME/var/lib/splunk. Before data can be searched, it needs to be indexed, a process we describe here.

There are two ways to create an index, through the Splunk portal or by creating an indexes.conf file. You will be shown here how to create an index using the Splunk portal, but you should realize that when you do that, it simply generates an indexes.conf file.

You will be creating an index called wineventlogs to store Windows Event Logs. To do this, take the following steps:

1. In the Splunk navigation bar, go to **Settings**.
2. In the **Data** section, click on **Indexes**, which will take you to the Indexes page.
3. Click on **New Index**.

4. Now fill out the information for this new index as seen in the following screenshot, carefully going through steps 1 to 4.
5. Be sure to **Save** when you are done.

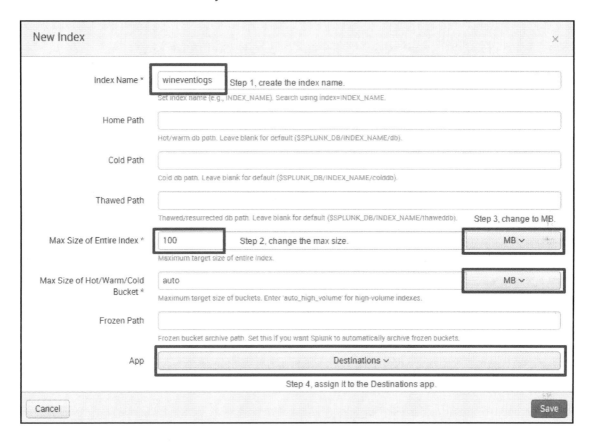

You will now see the new index in the list as shown here:

The preceding steps have created a new `indexes.conf` file. Now go ahead and inspect this file. In your administrator command prompt (assuming that you are at the root of the C: drive), type the following command:

```
C:\> notepad c:\splunk\etc\apps\destinations\local\indexes.conf
```

Every index has specific settings of its own. Here is how your index looks when automatically configured by the portal. In production environments, this is how Splunk administrators manage the indexes. Note that the max size value of 100 that you specified is also indicated in the configuration.

```
[wineventlogs]
coldPath = $SPLUNK_DB\wineventlogs\colddb
homePath = $SPLUNK_DB\wineventlogs\db
maxTotalDataSizeMB = 100
thawedPath = $SPLUNK_DB\wineventlogs\thaweddb
```

The complete `indexes.conf` documentation can be found at `http://docs.splunk.com/Documentation/Splunk/latest/admin/indexesconf`.

Buckets

You may have noticed that there is a certain pattern in this configuration file, in which folders are broken into three locations: `coldPath`, `homePath`, and `thawedPath`. This is a very important concept in Splunk. An index contains compressed raw data and associated index files that can be spread out into age-designated directories. Each piece of this index directory is called a **bucket**.

A bucket moves through several stages as it ages. In general, as your data gets older (think colder) in the system, it is pushed to the next bucket. And, as you can see in the following list, the thawed bucket contains data that has been resurrected from an archive. Here is a breakdown of the buckets in relation to each other:

- **hot**: This is newly indexed data and open for writing (`hotPath`)
- **warm**: This is data rolled from hot with no active writing (`warmPath`)
- **cold**: This is data rolled from warm (`coldPath`)
- **frozen**: This is data rolled from cold and deleted by default but it can be archived (`frozenPath`)
- **thawed**: This is data restored from the archive (`thawedPath`)

Now going back to the `indexes.conf` file, realize that the `homePath` will contain the hot and warm buckets, the `coldPath` will contain the cold bucket, and the `thawedPath` will contain any restored data from the archive. This means you can put buckets in different locations to efficiently manage disk space.

In production environments, Splunk admins never use the portal to generate indexes. They make their changes in the `indexes.conf` file. It is best practice to always use a temporary index for new data that you are unfamiliar with. Go ahead and create a new index stanza in `indexes.conf` with the following information:

```
[temp]
coldPath = $SPLUNK_DB\temp\colddb
homePath = $SPLUNK_DB\temp\db
maxTotalDataSizeMB = 100
thawedPath = $SPLUNK_DB\temp\thaweddb
```

1. Click on **Save**.
2. **Exit** the `indexes.conf` file when you are done.
3. Restart Splunk, which you must do for this change to take effect.
4. After restarting Splunk, go to the
   `http://localhost:8000/en-US/manager/destinations/data/indexes`
   page to confirm that the new index named `temp` has been created.

Data inputs

As you may have noticed, any configuration you make in the Splunk portal corresponds to a `*.conf` file written to the disk. The same goes for the creation of data inputs; it creates a file called `inputs.conf`. Now that you have an index to store your machine's Windows Event Logs, let us go ahead and create a data input for it, with the following steps:

1. Go to the Splunk home page.
2. Click on your Destinations app. Make sure you are in the Destinations app before you execute the next steps.
3. In the Splunk navigation bar, select **Settings**.
4. Under the **Data** section, click on **Data inputs**.

5. On the **Data inputs** page, click on the **Local event log collection** type as shown in the following screenshot:

6. In the next page select the **Application** and **System** log types.
7. Change the index to `wineventlog`. Compare your selections with the following screenshot:

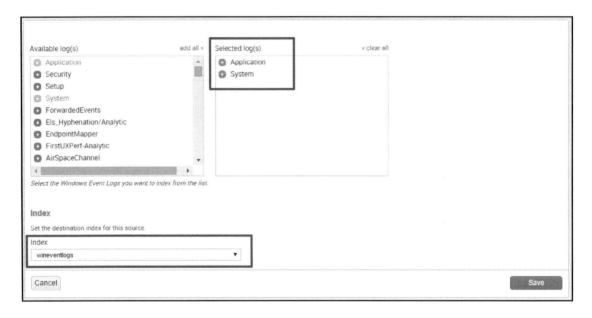

8. Click **Save**.

9. On the next screen, confirm that you have successfully created the data input, as shown in the following screenshot:

Before we proceed further, let's make sure that the data input works. To do so, follow these steps:

1. Go to the Destinations search page: `http://localhost:8000/en-US/app/destinations/search`.
2. In the search window, run the following Splunk search query:

```
SPL> index=wineventlogs | top sourcetype
```

3. Check the search results to see that there are now two actively-indexed source types in your Splunk system, that is, **WinEventLog:System** and **WinEventLog:Application**.
4. View the events of each of these source types by clicking the source type name and selecting **View events** as shown in the following screenshot:

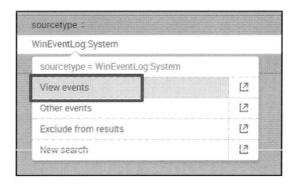

We have introduced a new concept here called **source types**. A source type is a type of classification of data that has been automatically made for you when you created the data input through the Splunk portal. In the same index, due to the steps we just took precedingly, Splunk internally classified the **System** and **Applications** event logs so you can access the events separately. There will be more about source types in Chapter 3, *Search Processing Language*.

Go ahead and inspect the `inputs.conf` file:

1. In an administrator prompt, open the file with this command:

   ```
   C:\> notepad c:\splunk\etc\apps\destinations\local\inputs.conf
   ```

2. Compare your results with this generated `inputs.conf` file:

   ```
   [WinEventLog://Application]
   checkpointInterval = 5
   current_only = 0
   disabled = 0
   index = wineventlogs
   start_from = oldest

   [WinEventLog://System]
   checkpointInterval = 5
   current_only = 0
   disabled = 0
   index = wineventlogs
   start_from = oldest
   ```

You can add directly into the `inputs.conf` file by following the same format. Use the temp index for testing. Here is an example input file based on a log file that is generated by the Splunk application. Note that this is going to be redundant to what is already being ingested through the `_internal` index and will only serve as an example.

```
[monitor://C:\Splunk\var\log\splunk\eventgen.log]
disabled = 0
sourcetype = eventgen
index = temp
```

Changes to the `inputs.conf` may require a Splunk restart. You can access that information with the following search command:

```
SPL> index=temp sourcetype=eventgen
```

The complete documentation for the `inputs.conf` file can be found at https://docs.splunk.com/Documentation/Splunk/latest/Admin/Inputsconf.

If you closely followed the instructions in this book, you should now have exactly four data sources in your very own Splunk system that will be used in the remainder of the book. This is how you can query raw data from these data sources.

Splunk events and fields

All throughout this chapter you have been running Splunk search queries that have returned data. It is important to understand what events and fields are before we go any further, for an understanding of these is essential to comprehending what happens when you run Splunk on the data.

In Splunk, a single piece of data is known as an **event** and is like a record, such as a log file or other type of input data. An event can have many different attributes or fields or just a few attributes or fields. When you run a successful search query, you will see that it brings up events from the data source. If you are looking at live streaming data, events can come in very quickly through Splunk.

Every event is given a number of default fields. For a complete listing, go to `http://docs.s plunk.com/Documentation/Splunk/6.3.2/Data/Aboutdefaultfields`. We will now go through some of these default fields.

- **Timestamp**: A timestamp is applied at the exact time the event is indexed in Splunk. Usually, Splunk can figure out what timestamp to assign from the raw data it receives. For example, as a shopper clicks the final purchase button on an e-commerce website, data is collected about precisely when the sale occurred. Splunk can usually automatically detect this from the raw data.
- **Host**: The host field tells us what the hostname, IP address, or full domain name of the data is.
- **Index**: The index field describes where the event is located, giving the specific name of the index.
- **Source and sourcetype**: The source field tells us where the data came from, specifically the file, data stream, or other data input. The sourcetype is the format of the data input from which the data came. Common sourcetypes are `access_combined`, `access_custom`, and `cisco_syslog`.
- **Linecount**: The linecount is simply the number of lines contained in the event.

These default fields are name/value pairings that are added to events when Splunk indexes data. Think of fields as a quick way to categorize and group events. Fields are the primary constituents of all search queries. In later chapters you will learn more about fields and how to create custom fields from events.

Extracting new fields

Most raw data that you will encounter will have some form of structure. Just like a CSV (comma-separated value file) or a web log file, it is assumed that each entry in the log corresponds to some sort of format. Splunk 6.3+ makes custom field extraction very easy, especially for delimited files. Let's take the case of our Eventgen data and look at the following example. If you look closely, the _raw data is actually delimited by white spaces:

```
2016-01-21 21:19:20:013632 130.253.37.97 GET /home - 80 - 10.2.1.33
"Mozilla/5.0 (iPad; U; CPU OS 4_3_3 like Mac OS X; en-us)
AppleWebKit/533.17.9 (KHTML, like Gecko) Version/5.0.2 Mobile/8J3
Safari/6533.18.5" 200 0 0 186 3804
```

Since there is a distinct separation of fields in this data, we can use Splunk's out-of-the-box field extraction tool to automatically classify these fields. In your Destinations app Search page, run the following search command:

```
SPL> index=main sourcetype=access_custom
```

This sourcetype `access_custom` refers to a type of file format that is generated by a server as it creates a web log file. After the data populates, click on the **Extract New Fields** link in the left column of the page as shown in the following screenshot:

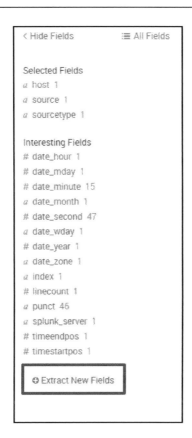

In the resulting **Extract Fields** page, select one of the events that is shown in the _raw events area. Try to select an entry with the longest text. As soon as you do this, the text will appear highlighted at the top of the page, as per the following screenshot:

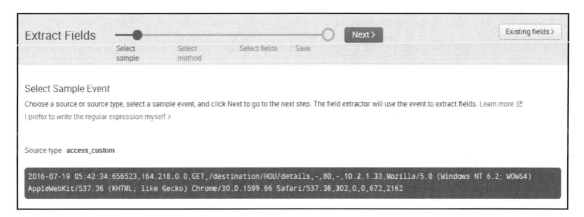

Click on the **Next** button to proceed. In the page that appears, click on the **Delimiters** icon as indicated in the following screenshot:

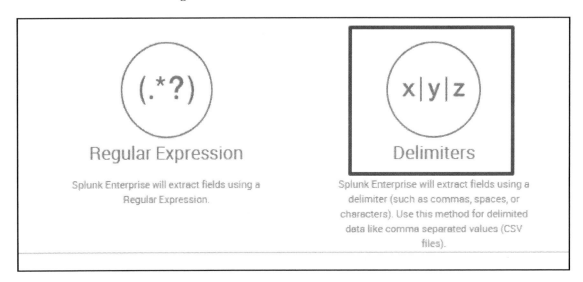

Click on **Next**. On the next page, click on the **Comma** delimiter as shown in the following screenshot:

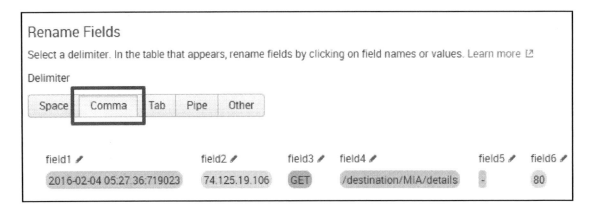

As soon as you select the **Comma** delimiter, Splunk will automatically allow you to modify each field and add a label to it. Click on the pencil icon for each field to input the label. When you're done, click on the **Rename Field** icon. For example, to edit **field3**, use the following screenshot:

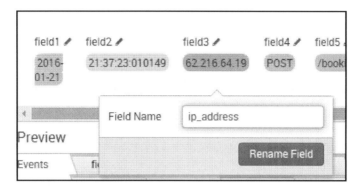

Do the same for the remaining fields using the following guide. These fields will be needed in future chapters. You can skip those that are not included in the following list:

- **field1**: datetime
- **field2**: client_ip
- **field3**: http_method
- **field4**: http_uri
- **field8**: server_ip
- **field9**: http_user_agent
- **field10**: http_status_code
- **field14**: http_response_time

When you have completed the preceding task, click on **Next** to proceed. In the next window, label the **Extractions Name** as **eventgen** and select the **All apps** permission type. Refer to the following screenshot:

Click on **Finish** to complete the process. Now that you have extracted new fields, these will now be readily available in your search queries as exemplified below. In the next chapter, you will be shown how to use these new fields to filter search results. An example of the kind of search you can do on them is shown here:

```
SPL> index=main | top http_uri
```

If you want to go ahead and try this out now, just to prove that you have already made changes that will help you to understand the data you are bringing in, be our guest!

Summary

In this chapter, we learned about some terms that need to be understood about big data, such as what the terms streaming data, data latency, and data sparseness mean. We also covered the types of data that can be brought into Splunk. Then we studied what an index is, made an index for our data, and put in data from our Destinations app. We talked about what fields and events are. And finally, we saw how to extract fields from events and name them so that they can be more useful to us. In the chapters to come, we'll learn more about these important features of Splunk.

3
Search Processing Language

In the previous chapters, you learned how to collect and index data to prepare it for searching, and how to do a simple search. In this chapter, we will cover more about how to use search and other commands to analyze our data. In a nutshell, we will cover the following topics:

- Anatomy of a search
- Search pipeline
- Time modifiers
- Filtering searches
- Search command-`stats`
- Search command-`top`/`rare`
- Search commands-`chart` and `timechart`
- Search command-`eval`
- Search command-`rex`

Anatomy of a search

Search Processing Language (**SPL**), a special-purpose processing language, was developed to enable fast searching on machine-generated data that has been indexed into Splunk. The language was originally set up to be based on Unix piping and **Standard Query Language** (**SQL**). We'll explain piping later. SQL is the language most widely used to query databases. The Search Processing Language (SPL, as opposed to SQL) is a library of all search processing commands and their functions, arguments, and clauses. With a search command you can group different events, filter data based on a constraint, extract fields using regular expressions, perform statistical calculations, and other tasks.

Let us dissect a search query so you can understand exactly how it works. This will also help you to understand what pipes are. As you will see, a pipe basically takes the data that has come from an earlier step and after it has been acted on, filtered, or extracted, sends it on to the next step in processing.

We'll use the Destinations app here to show you a simple example:

1. Go to the Splunk home page.
2. Click on your Destinations app.
3. In your Destinations app's **Search** page, type in the following:

```
SPL> index=_internal sourcetype=splunk* | top limit=5 name
     | sort - name
```

The following diagram will allow you to visualize the data as it goes through one delimiting pipe (|) and another; in this case, from the internal index of Splunk, to limiting it to the top five names, to sorting by name, which then gets sent to the **Final Results** table. We will go through this step by step, as shown in the following screenshot:

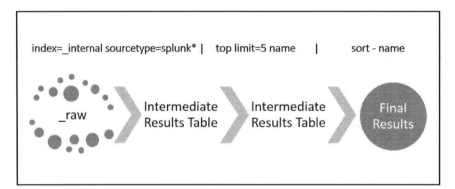

Search pipeline

The arrows in the preceding visualization, each of which represents a pipe, mean that the resulting data from the previous command will be used against the next command in the series. To fully understand this command, let's go through the pipes one by one. Type the following commands in succession into the search window, but pause in every one of them and observe how the data changes.

The following command will display the raw events:

```
SPL> index=_internal sourcetype=splunk*
```

This command used the raw events in the previous results table, keyed them on the name field, tabulated it by the number of events that the particular field has, then limited the result to five:

```
SPL> index=_internal sourcetype=splunk* | top limit=5 name
```

Finally, the results table of the | `top` command is passed on to another command | `sort` for sorting transformation.

```
SPL> index=_internal sourcetype=splunk* | top limit=5 name | sort - name
```

This chaining of commands is called the **search pipeline**.

Time modifiers

Every time you execute a search, always be aware that you are running a query against a set of data that is bound by date and time. The time-range picker is on the right side of the search bar. Splunk comes with predetermined time modifiers, as seen in the following screenshot. You can also use the time-range picker to set up a custom date/time range or other advanced ranges (https://docs.splunk.com/Splexicon:Timerangepicker):

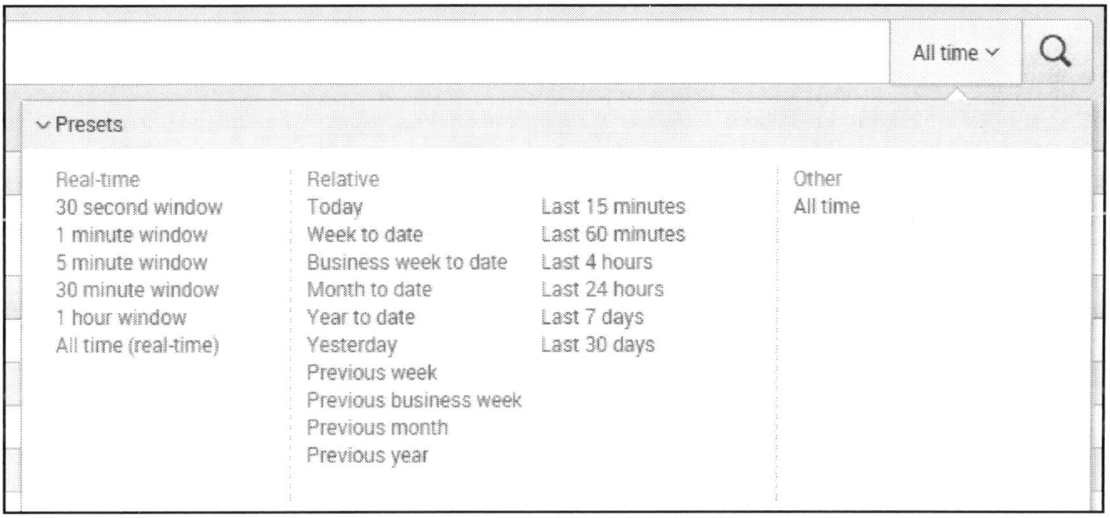

There are two types of time modifier: real-time and relative. In the preceding screenshot, the predetermined real-time modifiers are in the leftmost column, and the relative time modifiers are in the middle column.

Real-time modifiers mean that Splunk will run an ongoing, real-time search based on the specified time. For example, a real-time search that is in a 5-minute window will continuously display data within the last five minutes. If new data comes in, it will push out the oldest event within the time frame.

Real-time searches are resource-intensive. Use them sparingly. Other ways to efficiently show real-time data will be shown in later chapters.

Relative time modifiers are just that; they collect data based on relative time measures, and will find data within the specified timeframe.

What you do not see when you are using the time modifier drop-down is that in the background, Splunk is defining the earliest time and the latest time in specific variables.

The **last 15 minutes** preset, for example, is equivalent to this SPL modifier:

```
SPL> earliest=-15m latest=now
```

The presets built into Splunk automatically insert the `latest=now` modifier. Run this search command in your Destinations app **Search** bar:

```
SPL> index=main earliest=-30m latest=now | timechart count span=5m
```

Notice that even if you have not changed the time modifier selected in the drop-down menu (which will not change unless you use it), the data will show that your earliest event is 30 minutes ago and your last data is recent. In other words, what you put in the search bar overrides the time modifier drop-down menu.

You can use a number of alternative ways to identify each of the time units; the most commonly supported time units listed by Splunk are:

- **Second**: s, sec, secs, second, seconds
- **Minute**: m, min, minute, minute, minutes
- **Hour**: h, hr, hrs, hour, hours
- **Day**: d, day, days
- **Week**: w, week, weeks
- **Month**: mon, month, months

- **Quarter**: q, qtr, qtrs, quarter, quarters
- **Year**: y, yr, yrs, year, years

Filtering search results

Splunk is currently one of the best enterprise search engines, that is, a search engine that can serve the needs of any size organization currently on the market. Using a search command, you can filter your results using key phrases just the way you would with a Google search. Here are some examples for you to try out:

```
SPL> index=main /booking/confirmation
```

The preceding filters search results and only shows those with /booking/confirmation in the _raw data.

You may also add further filters by adding another phrase. It is very important to note, however, that by default, Splunk will assume that your phrases are logically chained based on an AND operator. For example:

```
SPL> index=main /booking 200
```

The preceding line of code is equivalent to the following:

```
SPL> index=main /booking AND 200
```

Similarly, you can use the OR operator to find data based on multiple filters. The following command will return all events with /booking or /destinations in the text. It is important to remember that an OR operator will always give you at least as many (or more) events than an AND operator, and AND is the default operator:

```
SPL> index=main /booking OR /destinations
```

Like any mathematical operation, you may also use parentheses to group conditions:

```
SPL> index=main (/booking OR /destinations) AND 200
```

If you have a phrase that has white space in it, it is best practice to enclose it with quotation marks, as seen in the following example:

```
SPL> index=main "iPhone OS"
```

You may also filter search results using fields. Fields are case-sensitive and a search using a specified field is generally faster than a full text search. Filtering using fields will only work if there is a defined field. In Chapter 2, *Bringing in Data*, you extracted new fields from the eventgen data source. Let's use that now to filter search results using custom fields:

```
SPL> index=main method=GET url="/home"
```

You can use this concept to combine data even if it comes from different indexes. Here is a query that shows the concepts we have discussed so far. Although the following query will result in a data set that will not make any sense, we include it to show how to combine data from different indexes:

```
SPL> (index=wineventlogs OR index=main) LogName=Application OR /booking
```

Search command – stats

The most common use of the stats command is to get a count of the total number of events that are the product of a search. To see how this works, run the following search query. Notice that the pipe that precedes the stats command filters the data that will be included in the final count:

```
SPL> index=main earliest=-30m latest=now | stats count
```

The preceding query will result in a single number that represents the total of all events within the given time modifier. Change the time modifier and the number should be reduced:

```
SPL> index=main earliest=-15m latest=now | stats count
```

You may be wondering where the count came from. The true format of a stats command is stats function(X). This asks the system to return the result of the function based on the field X. When the function count is used without parentheses, Splunk assumes that you are looking for the count of all events in the given search.

The stats command becomes a very powerful tool especially when you need to group counts by fields. Here is an example:

```
SPL> index=main  | stats count by method
```

This will result in two rows of data that will show the counts of the GET and the POST methods, as shown in the following screenshot. These are two methods that are used in HTTP (website communication rules for client and server) to ask for information (GET) and submit data (POST):

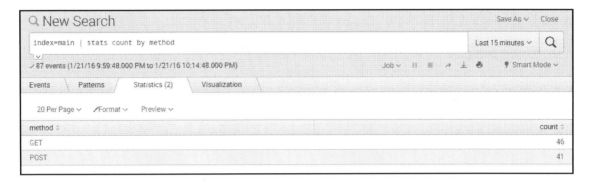

You can also use the avg(X) function to get the average value of all the events based on URLs. Here is an example that you can use:

```
SPL> index=main | stats count by url | stats avg(count)
```

Some of the widely used stats functions are:

- avg(X): Returns the average of the values of the field X
- dc(X): Returns the count of distinct values of the field X
- max(X): Returns the maximum value of the field X
- min(X): Returns the minimum value of the field X
- perc<X>(Y): Returns the Xth percentile of the field X, for example perc95(X)
- sum(X): Returns the sum of the values of the field X

 To learn more about the other stats functions, go to http://docs.splunk. com/Documentation/Splunk/latest/SearchReference/CommonStatsFun ctions.

Search command – top/rare

A quick way to get a summarized table based on fields is by using the `top` and `rare` commands. Run this search command:

```
SPL> index=main | top url
```

Notice that the result automatically grouped the URLs by count, calculated the percentage of each row against the whole data set, and sorted them by count in descending order. You can see a sample result in the following screenshot:

url ≑	count ≑	percent ≑
/booking/reservation	18	20.224719
/booking/confirmation	17	19.101124
/home	14	15.730337
/auth	13	14.606742
/destination/city/details	10	11.235955
/booking/payment	9	10.112360
/destinations/search	8	8.988764

You may further tweak this search command by adding command options such as `limit` and `showperc`. Say, for example, you only want to see the top five URLs but you do not want to see the percent column. This is the command to achieve that:

```
SPL> index=main | top url limit=5 showperc=false
```

Now try the same commands, but use `rare` instead of `top`. The term `rare` will find those events that are the most unlikely ones. This can be a useful qualifier to use for determining outliers or unusual cases that may be due to data entry errors.

Search commands – chart and timechart

The `chart` command is an aggregation command that provides output in tabular or chartable format. It is a very important command that is used for many different types of visualization. Notice that if you run the following search query, it is identical to the output of the `stats` command:

```
SPL> index=main | chart count by method
```

For all basic purposes, you can use `stats` and `chart` interchangeably. However, there will be differences in how `stats` and `chart` group data together. It will be up to you to determine which one is your intended result. To show the differences, here are some examples:

SPL> index=main | stats count by method url

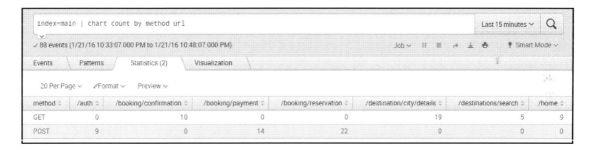

SPL> index=main | chart count by method url

method	/auth	/booking/confirmation	/booking/payment	/booking/reservation	/destination/city/details	/destinations/search	/home
GET	0	10	0	0	19	5	9
POST	9	0	14	22	0	0	0

The `timechart` command, on the other hand, creates a time series chart with statistical aggregation of the indicated fields. This command is widely used when creating different types of chart. The most common use of `timechart` is for examining the trends of metrics over time for visualizations including line charts, column charts, bar charts, and area charts, among others:

SPL> index=main earliest=-4h latest=now | timechart span=15m count by url

An important option that is part of the `timechart` command is `span`. The span essentially determines how it will bucket the data based on time slices. `span=15m` means it will aggregate the data and slice it every 15 minutes.

The statistical result of the command looks like this:

_time ⬦	/auth ⬦	/booking/confirmation ⬦	/booking/payment ⬦	/booking/reservation ⬦	/destination/city/details ⬦
2016-01-21 18:50:00	1	0	1	1	0
2016-01-21 18:55:00	13	9	5	9	6
2016-01-21 19:00:00	9	13	9	9	4
2016-01-21 19:05:00	11	11	4	13	10
2016-01-21 19:10:00	6	13	6	10	9

Although admittedly the preceding data looks dull, this very same information, when viewed in the **Visualizations** tab, looks much more interesting, as seen in the following screenshot. There will be more on creating dashboard panels and dashboards in `Chapter 6`, *Panes of Glass*:

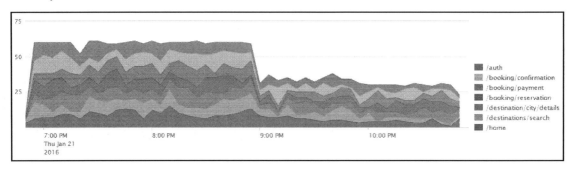

Search command – eval

The `eval` command is perhaps the most advanced and powerful command in SPL. It allows you to store the resulting value of the `eval` operation in a field. A myriad of functions available today can be used with `eval`. Let us try some of the simpler and more common ones.

The simplest type of `eval` command performs a simple calculation and stores it in the newly created field. For example, if you want to create the `new_salary` field, which adds together `old_salary` plus a field named `raise`, it would look like this (but don't try this, as there are no such fields in our data):

```
SPL> eval new_salary = old_salary + raise
```

There are also countless functions that can be used effectively with `eval`. Later we discuss some of them:

```
SPL> round(X, Y)
```

Run the search command below, then modify it to include the `eval` function `round(X, Y)`. Watch how the percent column values were transformed as they are rounded to the nearest integer with two decimal values:

```
SPL> index=main | top url

     index=main | top url | eval percent=round(percent, 2)

     upper(X)
```

Use this function to transform the URL strings into uppercase:

```
SPL> index=main | top url

     index=main | top url | eval url=upper(url)

     case(X, "Y", ...)
```

The `case` function is especially useful when transforming data based on a Boolean condition. If X is true, then assign to the variable the string Y. Here is one example:

```
SPL> index=main | top url showperc=false
     | eval Tag=case(url=="/home", "Home", url="/auth", "Auth")
```

The resulting table shows that a new column called `Tag` has been created and all instances of /home have been marked as `Home` and all instances of /auth have been marked as `Auth`:

url ⇕	count ⇕	Tag ⇕
/destination/city/details	65	
/booking/reservation	62	
/booking/payment	55	
/booking/confirmation	53	
/auth	52	Auth
/home	47	Home
/destinations/search	28	

Search command – rex

The rex or regular expression command is extremely useful when you need to extract a field during search time that has not already been extracted automatically. The rex command even works in multi-line events. The following sample command will get all the versions of the Chrome browser that are defined in the highlighted User Agent string part of the following raw data. Let's say this is your raw data, and you need to get the highlighted value:

```
016-07-21 23:58:50:227303,96.32.0.0,GET,/destination/LAX/details,-,80,
-,10.2.1.33,Mozilla/5.0 (Macintosh; Intel Mac OS X 10_8_5)
AppleWebKit/537.36 (KHTML; like Gecko) Chrome/29.0.1547.76
Safari/537.36,500,0,0,823,3053
```

You can use this search command to get it:

```
SPL> index=main | rex field=http_user_agent
     "Chrome/(?<Chrome_Version>.+?)?Safari" | top Chrome_Version
```

The rex command extracted a field called Chrome_Version during the search and made it available for all succeeding commands. The results are shown in the following screenshot:

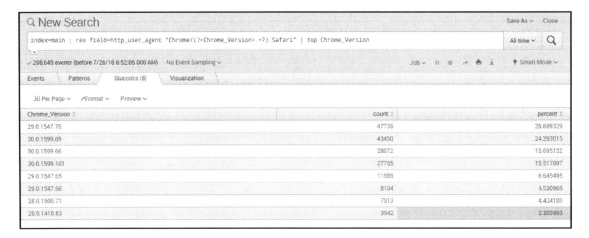

Summary

In this chapter, we introduced you to the SPL. You have learned that the search pipeline is crucial in the transformation of data as it is piped between search commands and eventually to the final results table. We also introduced you to time modifiers and how to filter search results. Lastly, you were introduced to multiple search commands that are commonly used. In `Chapter 5`, *Data Optimization, Reports, Alerts, and Accelerating Searches*, we will go on to use our search processing skills to create useful reports and learn about developing alerts that will increase organizational efficiency and prevent errors. We will also learn more about how to best optimize our searches.

4
Data Models and Pivot

Splunk data models and the Pivot tool are key features that enable users to generate statistical data and charts without the complexity of the **Search Processing Language** (SPL). A data model is a hierarchical mapping of data based on search results. It is analogous to the concept of schemas in a relational database. The output of the search queries associated with the data model can be visualized as a set of rows and columns in a spreadsheet. The data is further subdivided by attributes, which are essentially extracted fields that are similar to those discussed in Chapter 2, *Bringing in Data*. Since data models are essentially rows and columns of data, we can use them to generate a Pivot table to provide a myriad of different, summarized results.

In this chapter, we will learn how to:

- Create a data model
- Enable acceleration for the data model
- Make a Pivot table
- Visualize data using area charts, pie charts, and single value with trend sparklines

Creating a data model

Before you can create a Pivot table, you need to develop a set of rows and columns through the creation of a data model. To do this, perform the following steps:

1. In the Destinations app, click on the Pivot link in the top menu. Observe the **Select a Data Model** page, which will be empty until you have created your first data model.

2. Click on the **Manage Data Models** button in the upper-right corner of the screen to proceed.

3. In the **Data Models** screen, click on **New Data Model**.

4. Give your new data model a title and ID and ensure that it is created in the Destinations app. Refer to the following screenshot as a guide:

5. Click on **Create**. You are now in the Destinations data model editing page.

6. Click on the **Add Object** dropdown and select **Root Event**. The concept of data model hierarchy is now in play. The **Root Event** or **Root Search** is the base search that will populate the data for the entire data model tree.

7. Populate the **Root Event** with the fields seen in the following screenshot. We want to create a data model for our Eventgen data so we use `index=main` as the primary constraint:

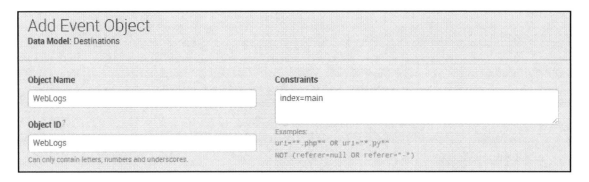

8. Click on **Preview** to ensure that the `index=main` search returns the expected results. Click on **Save**.

After saving the root event, there will be attributes that will be created as default. Because data models respect hierarchies, these initial attributes will be inherited by all child objects. Attributes or fields that are generic to all data regardless of search constraints need to be created in the root object.

Adding attributes to objects

There are different ways to add an attribute to an object. In this book we will utilize extracted attributes based on fields and regular expressions. Go ahead and carry out these steps:

1. Click on the **Add Attribute** dropdown and select **Auto-Extracted**.
2. Scroll down the list of auto-extracted fields and select the fields that we have manually extracted in `Chapter 2`, *Bringing in Data*, as listed and shown in the bullet list followed by the screenshot:
   - `http_method`
   - `http_port`
   - `http_response_time`
   - `http_status_code`
   - `http_uri`
   - `http_user_agent`

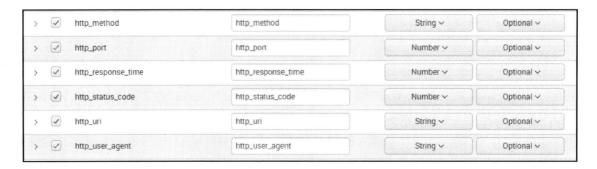

3. If you look closely, you'll see Splunk has automatically classified the attributes based on its assumed data type (for instance **String** for `client_ip` and **Number** for `http_status_code`). You can do the same steps if you missed an attribute.

Your newly-added attributes are now in the **Extracted** section and will also be inherited by all child objects, as a child object in Splunk inherits the constraints and attributes of a parent object.

Creating child objects

To create a child object, do the following:

1. Select the **WebLogs** event, click on the **Add Object** dropdown, and select **Child**.
2. Populate the form with the following information. Click on **Save** to proceed.
    - **Object Name**: `Authenticated`
    - **Additional Constraints**: `http_uri="/auth"`
3. Click on **Preview** to review.
4. Click on **Save** to proceed.
5. Click on the **Authenticated** child object (under **WebLogs** in the upper left) and observe that all the attributes of the root object have been inherited.

Create more child objects of the root object, **WebLogs**:

Object name	Additional constraints
Booking Confirmation	`http_uri="/booking/confirmation"`
Booking Payment	`http_uri="/booking/payment"`
Destination Details	`http_uri="/destination/*/details"`
Destinations Search	`http_uri="/destinations/search"`

You now have five child objects that are differentiated by the pages viewed in your web log as shown in the following screenshot:

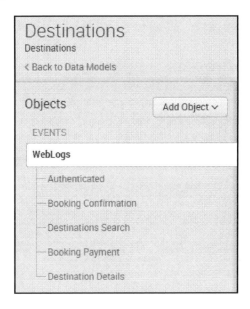

Creating an attribute based on a regular expression

Now we are going to create an attribute based on a regular expression, which is a specialized text string that describes a search pattern. What we want to do is extract the airport code that is part of the **Destination Details** URI:

```
http_uri="/destination/MIA/details"
```

To do this, we have to create an attribute in the **Destination Details** object. Take these steps:

1. Select the **Destination Details** object, click on the **Add Attribute** dropdown, and select **Regular Expression**.
2. In the **Regular Expression** field, type in the following text:

    ```
    /destination/(?<AirportCode>.+?)/details
    ```

3. Click on the blank area outside the text box to populate the **Attributes** field as shown in the following screenshot.
4. Change the display name to `Airport Code`:

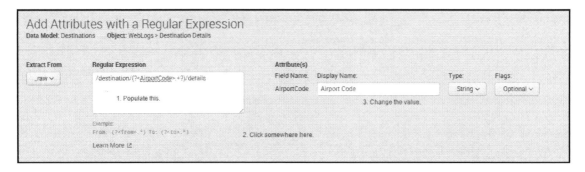

5. Click on **Preview** and make sure that the airport codes are highlighted in the events. You can also click the **Airport Code** tab to see them summarized. Also, click the **Non-Matches** button and ensure that no events are shown:

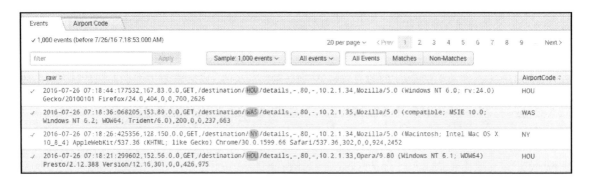

6. Click on **Save** to proceed.

Now that you have built your first data model, it is time to prepare it for use in Pivot. Here are the steps to perform:

1. Change the permission of the data model so all other Splunk users can use it in the context of the Destinations app. On the **Edit** dropdown, select **Edit Permissions**:

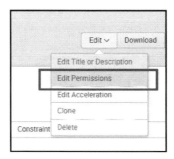

2. Change the permission of the data model so that it is available for the Destinations app. Click on **App** on the **Display For** button set.
3. Set the **Read** permission to **Everyone** and the **admin** group to **Write**:

4. Click on **Save** to continue. In the next section, we will introduce you to data model acceleration and how to enable it.

Data model acceleration

When you enable acceleration for a data model, Splunk internally summarizes the data defined by the data model in a given time range. This gives a tremendous boost to the search speed for your data model. There are a couple of things to remember when you enable data model acceleration:

1. Once you enable acceleration for a data model, you will no longer be able to edit the data model objects. Ensure that you have properly configured your child objects and attributes before you decide to accelerate. A huge data model may take some time to complete the acceleration process, so plan accordingly. You will only be able to edit the data model again if you disable the acceleration.

2. Select your summary range wisely. The summary range is the calculation time span that the acceleration will use against your data. The summary range can span 1 day, 7 days, 1 month, 3 months, 1 year, and so on. Search acceleration is based on time ranges. Only those that fall within the selected time range will be accelerated. If you need to accelerate for 5 days, then it is safe to select 7 days. However, if you run the report for 10 days, the searches beyond the selected acceleration range will execute at a normal speed.

3. Acceleration will take up disk space. A large data model with a lengthy summary range will occupy much more disk space than your current index.

In this exercise, you will enable data model acceleration with a summary range of 7 days.

You will want to follow these steps very carefully:

1. Once again in the **Edit** dropdown, select **Edit Acceleration**:

2. In the **Edit Acceleration** prompt, check the **Accelerate** box and select **7 Days** as your **Summary Range**. These options are seen in the following screenshot:

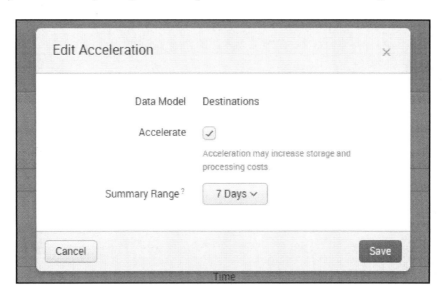

3. Click on **Save** to kick off the acceleration process. Notice that Splunk will issue a warning that the data model is locked and can no longer be edited unless you disable acceleration:

4. Let us check the status of the acceleration process. Go back to the **Data Models** main page and expand the **Destinations** data model by clicking the side > next to **Destinations**. You should see information that is similar to the following screenshot:

5. Under the **Acceleration** section, you will see a sizable amount of information about the state of your data model acceleration, such as the status, access count, size on disk, summary range, buckets, and the last time it got updated. It will take a couple of minutes until the acceleration is complete. Keep refreshing the page until the **Status** says **100.00% Completed**, as shown in the following screenshot:

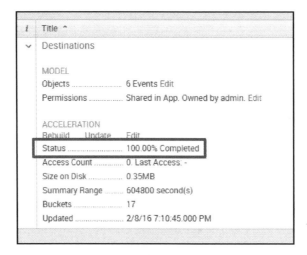

Now that the data model has been fully constructed and accelerated, it is time to use it with the Pivot Editor.

The Pivot Editor

Now we will begin to make a Pivot table; follow these directions:

1. Go back to the Destinations app and click on **Pivot** in the main menu.
2. This time, simply click on the **WebLogs** object. You will see a page as shown in the following screenshot with a count of all **WebLogs** data for **All Time**:

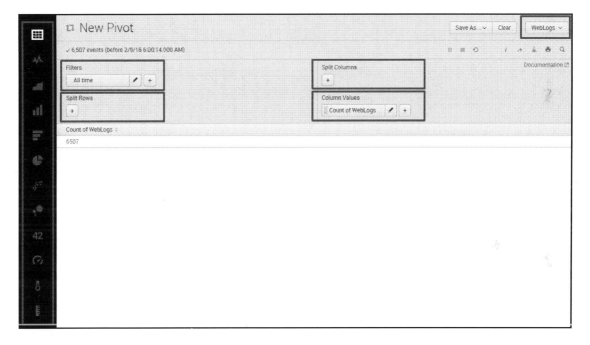

We have highlighted different sections in this page. The navigation bar icons to the left of the screen represent the different visualization modes. The default and topmost visualization is the statistics table. You will always first construct your statistics table before you go to any of the other visualizations.

The **time range** functions the same throughout Splunk. Always change it to something within the scope of your acceleration summary range (7 days in this case). **Filters** will allow you to narrow down your dataset based on object attributes.

Split Rows and **Split Columns** will allow you to change the orientation of your data based on **Time** and **Attribute**. The following screenshot shows you what attributes will appear on the **Split Columns** dropdown:

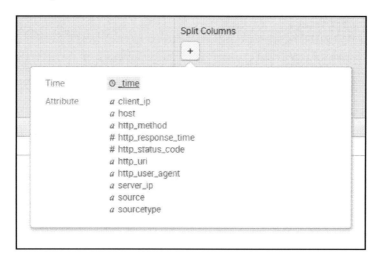

Column Values on the other hand will allow you to select an **Event** or **Attribute** based on **Time,** as shown in the following screenshot:

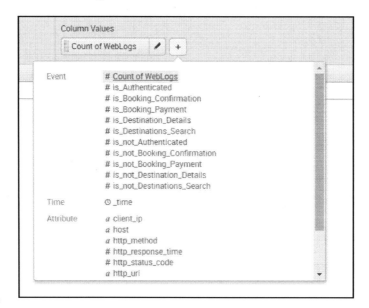

This will all look confusing at first so it is best to walk through it by means of examples.

In the upper-right corner of the page, you will see the scope of the Pivot. This is usually the object that you clicked when you first entered the Pivot Editor. Through this dropdown, you can switch to other data models and other objects, as shown in the following screenshot. It is also a shortcut for checking the status of acceleration:

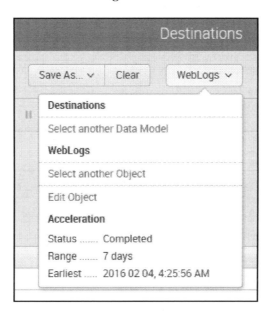

The Pivot Editor will always default to the **Count** of the object that was selected in the data model. That is why, in the results section, you see **Count of WebLogs**:

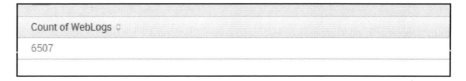

Creating a chart from a Pivot

Let us create a chart that will represent web traffic. **WebLogs** that have been generated by Eventgen are simulated data from a web application with varied status codes. Every line in the web log is a request from a web client (such as the browser or mobile device). In effect, the sum of all the requests and status codes equals the entire traffic of the web application.

To create a chart, do the following:

1. First, change the time range to **Last 7 days**.
2. Change **Split Rows** to **_time** and leave **Periods** as the default, as shown next. This is equivalent to using the `timechart` function in SPL without specifying a *span*. Opt out of **Totals** if you do not want the bottom row of your dataset to include the summation of the entire column. In this case, we do not need **Totals**, so **No** is selected:

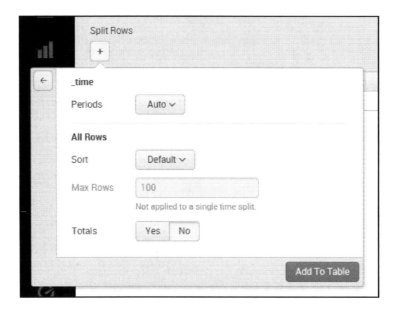

3. Click **Add To Table**. The results will change to show seven rows, with the sum of the **WebLogs** tallied in each row. In **Split Columns**, add the `http_status_code` attribute to split the columns based on `http_status_code`. There will be many options available to you to tweak your data set for the **Split Columns** function, but for now leave them as they are. The final selection of filters is shown in the following screenshot:

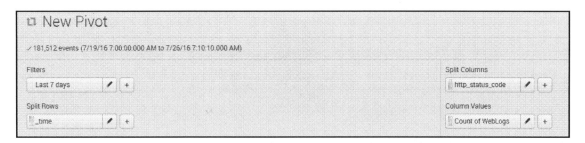

Your statistics table should have changed. The count per day has now been split based on the `http_status_code` attribute, as shown next. Since your data model is accelerated and you have selected the time filter that fits the summary range, the results should render almost instantaneously:

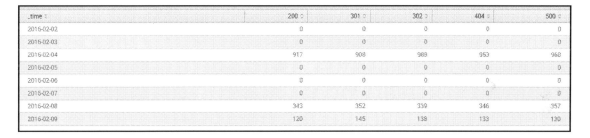

_time	200	301	302	404	500
2016-02-02	0	0	0	0	0
2016-02-03	0	0	0	0	0
2016-02-04	917	908	988	953	968
2016-02-05	0	0	0	0	0
2016-02-06	0	0	0	0	0
2016-02-07	0	0	0	0	0
2016-02-08	343	352	339	346	357
2016-02-09	120	145	138	133	130

Creating an area chart

Now that the statistics table has been populated with data, it is time to choose a visualization method:

1. Select the **Area** visualization tool in the left menu bar, as shown in the following screenshot:

The next page will show you an array of options that you can choose from to change the way your area chart behaves. Depending on how long you have been running Splunk on your machine, you should see a stacked area chart similar to the following screenshot:

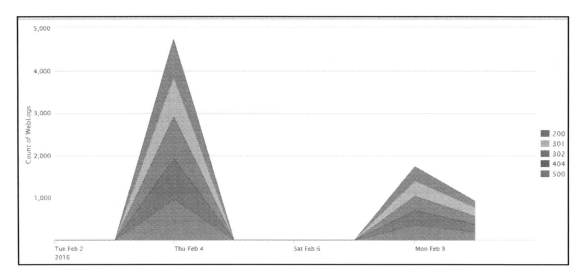

2. Let us change the look and feel of the area chart a little bit. In the **X-Axis (Time)** section, choose to **hide** the **Label**. This will remove the _time label on the *x* axis:

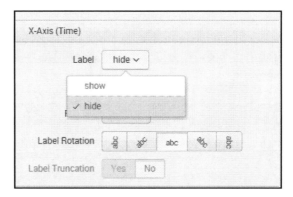

3. In the **Color (Areas)** section, let's move the **Legend Position** to the bottom, as shown in the following screenshot:

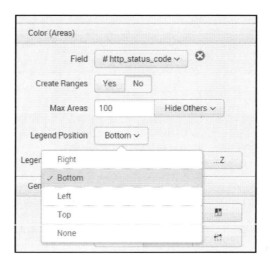

4. Your area chart is now ready to be saved as a Dashboard panel. Click on the **Save As** button and select **Dashboard Panel**.

5. Let us create a new dashboard called **Summary Dashboard**. Make sure you change the permission to **Shared in App**.

6. Finally, change the **Panel Title** to **Web Traffic per Day Last 7 Days**.

7. Click on **Save** to finish and click on **View Dashboard**. Use the following screenshot as a guide:

You now have a dashboard that is driven by the data model that you just created. It should look similar to what is shown here:

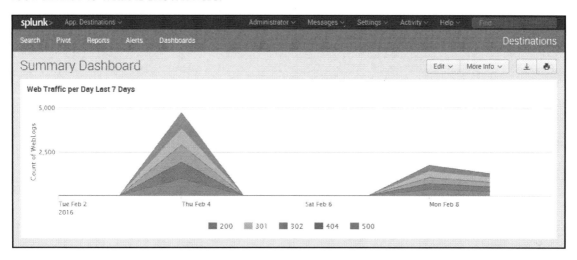

Creating a pie chart showing destination details by airport code

We will now create a pie chart that will show us the Destination Details by Airport Code. If you recall, at the beginning of this chapter we created a data model object and used a regular expression to extract the **Airport Code** as a field.

These instructions will help you to create a pie chart:

1. Go back to the Pivot Editor and this time, select **Destination Details**.
2. Change your time range to **Last 24 hours**.

3. In **Split Rows**, select **Airport Code**. Your Pivot Editor should now show something similar to the following screenshot:

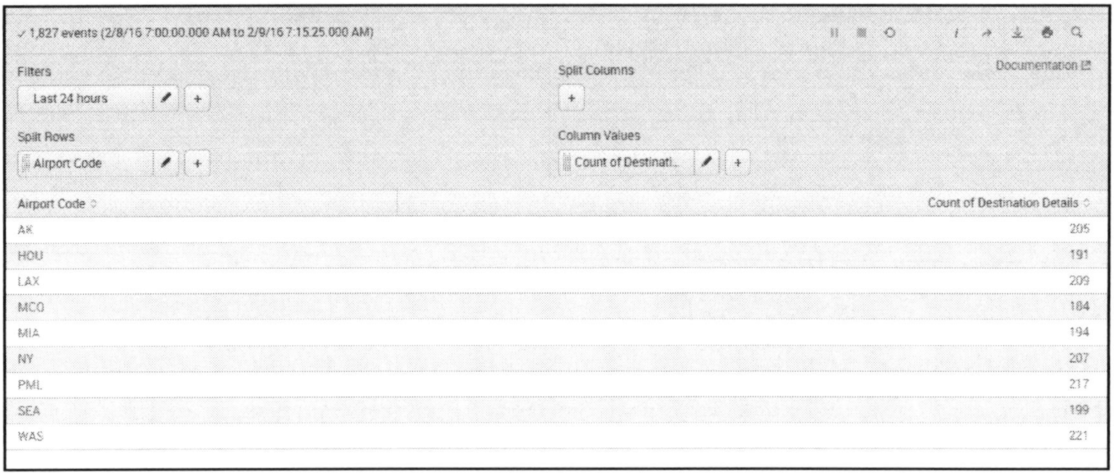
✓ 1,827 events (2/8/16 7:00:00.000 AM to 2/9/16 7:15:25.000 AM)
Filters
Last 24 hours
Split Columns
Documentation
Split Rows
Airport Code
Column Values
Count of Destinati...
Airport Code
Count of Destination Details
AK 205
HOU 191
LAX 209
MCO 184
MIA 194
NY 207
PML 217
SEA 199
WAS 221

4. This data is sufficient to generate a pie chart. Go ahead and click the **Pie Chart** icon on the navigation bar to the left:

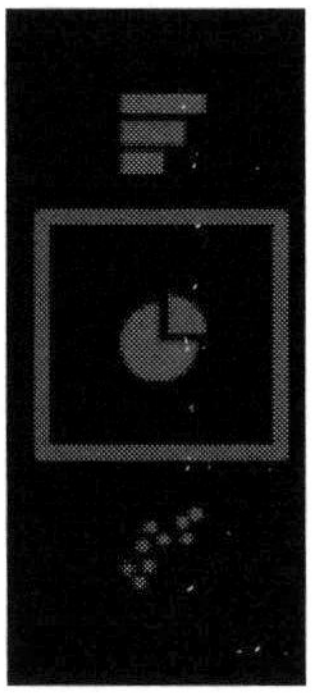

Without changing any other options, the pie chart appears. Splunk has rendered a chart subdividing the different airport codes in the last 24 hours:

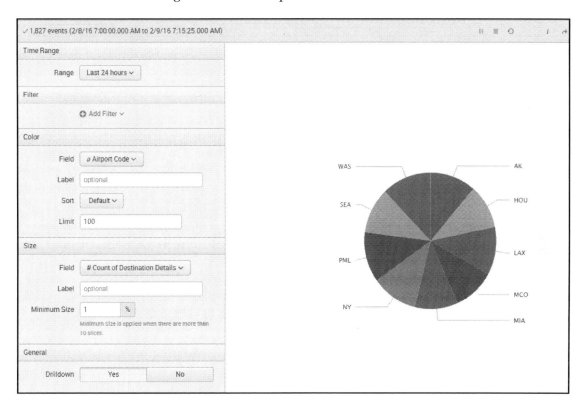

5. Add this to the **Summary Dashboard** by once again selecting **Save As** a **Dashboard panel**.
6. Click on the **Existing** button and select **Summary Dashboard**.
7. Give it this title: **Destinations Last 24 Hrs**.

8. Click on **Save** and go to your dashboard to see the end result:

Single value with trending sparkline

We will now use one of the cooler visualizations that Splunk has by default, the single value with trending sparkline.

1. Go back to Pivot and select **Booking Confirmation**.
2. Change your time range to **Last 24 hours**. That's all you need to do here.
3. Go ahead and click on the **Single Value** visualization option as indicated here:

4. The default is a big boring number. Let us spice it up. In the **Sparkline** section, click on **Add Sparkline** then select **_time**. Change the **Periods** to **Hours** as shown here:

5. Check it out; Splunk just gave you an awesome visualization with very little effort. It will now show you the number of **Booking Confirmations** since the start of the hour and will provide a number comparison from the hour before. It will also give you an upward or a downward arrow that depicts trends and will add a sparkline at the bottom of the number:

6. We're not done yet! Let us put even more life into it. In the **Color** section, click on **Yes** in **Use Colors**. In the **Color by** option, select **Trend**. Select the second option for **Color Mode**. Here is how the **Color** section looks now:

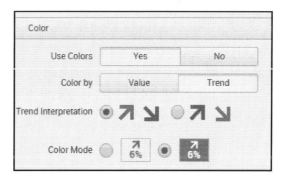

With those options selected, your visualization will have now changed to something similar to what you see next.

7. Finally, save this panel to the **Summary Dashboard** and label it as **Booking Confirmations**.

Rearranging your dashboard

Before going on, you can rearrange your dashboard so that it looks the way you want:

1. In the **Summary Dashboard**, click on the **Edit** button and select **Edit Panels**. This will convert the panels into widgets that you can drag around.
2. Change the final layout of your **Summary Dashboard** to look like the following screenshot. Click on **Done** once you have laid the widgets out in the correct orientation:

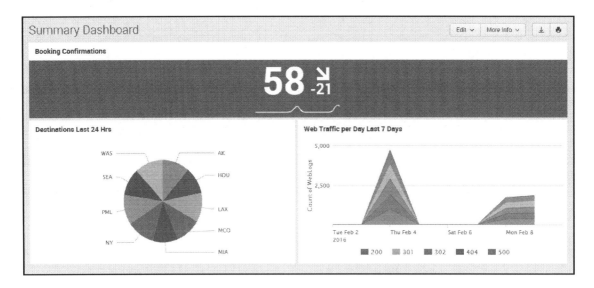

Summary

By now, you have familiarized yourself with data models and the Pivot Editor. In this chapter, we explained what data models are and how they are created. We walked you through how to create your data model objects based on a hierarchy. You also have learned that data models consist of attributes that can be inherited from the parent objects. You created an attribute by extracting a field using regular expression. We have also shown you how to use the Pivot Editor and create three different visualizations: area chart, pie chart, and single value with trend sparkline.

In the next chapter, Chapter 5, *Data Optimization, Reports, Alerts, and Accelerating Searches,* you will learn how to create and use these important Splunk tools as well as how to optimize searches.

5

Data Optimization, Reports, Alerts, and Accelerating Searches

Finding the data that you need in Splunk is relatively easy, as you have seen in the previous chapters. Doing the same thing repeatedly, however, requires that you employ techniques that make data retrieval faster. In Chapter 2, *Bringing in Data*, you have been shown how to use data fields and to make field extractions. In Chapter 4, *Data Models and Pivot*, you learned how to create data models. You will continue that journey in this chapter by learning how to classify your data using event types, enrich your data using lookups and workflow actions, and normalize your data using tags.

Once you have all these essentials in place, you will be able to easily create reports, alerts, and dashboards. This is where Splunk really shines and your hard work so far will pay off.

In this chapter, we will cover a wide range of topics that showcase ways to manage, analyze, and get results from data. These topics will help you learn to work more efficiently with data and gather better insights from it:

- Data classification with event types
- Data normalization with tags
- Data enrichment with lookups
- Creating reports
- Creating alerts
- The Custom Cron schedule

- Best practices in scheduling jobs
- Optimizing searches

Data classification with event types

When you begin working with Splunk every day, you will quickly notice that many things are repeatable. In fact, while going through this book, you may have seen that search queries can easily get longer and more complex. One way to make things easier and shorten search queries is to create event types. Event types are not the same as events; an event is just a single instance of data. An event type is a grouping or classification of events that meet the same criteria.

If you took a break between chapters, you will probably want to open up Splunk again. Then you will execute a search command:

1. Open up Splunk.
2. Click on your Destinations app.
3. Type in this query:

```
SPL> index=main http_uri=/booking/confirmation http_status_code=200
```

This data will return successful booking confirmations. Now say you want to search for this the next day. Without any data classification, you'll have to type the same search string as previously. Instead of tedious repetition, you can simplify your work by saving this search now as an event type. Follow these steps now:

1. In the **Save As** dropdown, select **Event Type**:

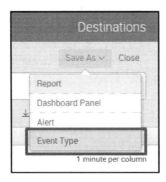

2. Label this new event type `good_bookings`.
3. Select a color that is best suited for the type of event; in this case, we will select **green**.
4. Select **5** as the priority. Priority here determines which style wins if there is more than one event type. One is the highest and 10 is the lowest.
5. Use the following screenshot as a guide, then click on **Save**:

Now let's create an event type for bad bookings:

1. Change the search query from `http_status_code=200` to `http_status_code=500`. The new query is as shown here:

SPL> index=main http_uri=/booking/confirmation http_status_code=500

2. Save this as an event type. This time, name it `bad_bookings` and opt for the color to be **red** and leaving **Priority** at **5**:

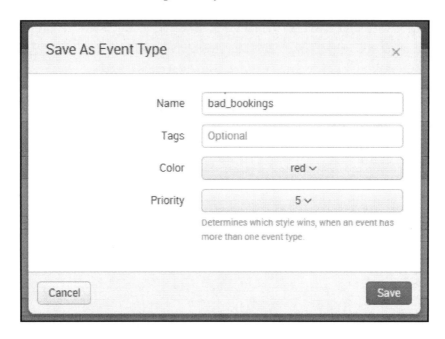

We have created the two event types we needed. Now let's see them in action:

1. Type the following query in the search input:

   SPL> eventtype=*bookings

2. Notice that the search results have now been color-coded based on the event type that you created. You can also just search for either `eventtype=good_bookings` or `eventtype=bad_bookings` to narrow down your search results.

3. Examine the following screenshot, which shows the results. The colors we have chosen make it easy to spot the types of booking. Imagine the time this saves a manager, who can instantly look for bad bookings. It's just one more way Splunk can make operations so much easier:

i	Time	Event
>	8/11/16 7:22:54.007 AM	2016-08-11 07:22:54:007028,143.115.0.0,GET,/booking/confirmation,-,80,-,10.2.1.34,Moz illa/5.0 (Windows NT 6.1) AppleWebKit/537.36 (KHTML; like Gecko) Chrome/30.0.1599.101 Safari/537.36,200,0,0,943,2280 host = www.destinations.com | source = web_log | sourcetype = access_custom
>	8/11/16 7:20:34.005 AM	2016-08-11 07:20:34:005312,208.176.0.0,GET,/booking/confirmation,-,80,-,10.2.1.34,Moz illa/5.0 (Windows NT 6.1; rv:24.0) Gecko/20100101 Firefox/24.0,500,0,0,797,3932 host = www.destinations.com | source = web_log | sourcetype = access_custom
>	8/11/16 7:19:12.053 AM	2016-08-11 07:19:12:053950,158.34.0.0,GET,/booking/confirmation,-,80,-,10.2.1.34,Mozi lla/5.0 (Macintosh; Intel Mac OS X 10_7_5) AppleWebKit/537.36 (KHTML; like Gecko) Chr ome/30.0.1599.101 Safari/537.36,200,0,0,561,3903 host = www.destinations.com | source = web_log | sourcetype = access_custom
>	8/11/16 7:16:08.736 AM	2016-08-11 07:16:08:736801,148.167.0.0,GET,/booking/confirmation,-,80,-,10.2.1.34,Moz illa/5.0 (Macintosh; Intel Mac OS X 10_8_3) AppleWebKit/537.36 (KHTML; like Gecko) Ch rome/30.0.1599.69 Safari/537.36,200,0,0,992,2490 host = www.destinations.com | source = web_log | sourcetype = access_custom
>	8/11/16 7:15:46.089 AM	2016-08-11 07:15:46:089896,136.203.0.0,GET,/booking/confirmation,-,80,-,10.2.1.33,Moz illa/5.0 (Macintosh; Intel Mac OS X 10_7_5) AppleWebKit/537.36 (KHTML; like Gecko) Ch rome/30.0.1599.101 Safari/537.36,500,0,0,719,3397 host = www.destinations.com | source = web_log | sourcetype = access_custom

Certain restrictions apply when creating event types. You cannot create an event type that consists of a piped command or subsearches. Only base commands can be saved as an event type.

Since the event type is now part of the search, you can then further manipulate data using piped commands, just like this:

```
SPL> eventtype=*bookings | stats count by eventtype
```

Create a few more event types now, using the following table as a guide:

Event type	Search command	Color
`good_payment`	`index=main http_uri=/booking/payment` `http_status_code=200`	green
`bad_payment`	`index=main http_uri=/booking/payment` `http_status_code=500`	red
`destination_details`	`index=main http_uri=/destination/*/details`	blue
`bad_logins`	`index=main http_uri=/auth` `http_status_code=500`	purple

Data normalization with tags

Tags in Splunk are useful for grouping events with related field values. Unlike event types, which are based on specified search commands, tags are created and mapped to specific fields. You can also have multiple tags assigned to the same field, and each tag can be assigned to that field for a specific reason.

The simplest use-case scenario when using tags is for classifying IP addresses. In our Eventgen logs, three IP addresses are automatically generated. We will create tags against these IP addresses that would allow us to classify them based on different conditions:

IP address	Tags
`10.2.1.33`	`main`, `patched`, `east`
`10.2.1.34`	`main`, `patched`, `west`
`10.2.1.35`	`backup`, `east`

In our server farm of three servers, we are going to group them by purpose, patch status, and geolocation. We will achieve this using tags, as shown in the following steps:

1. Begin by using the following search command:

   ```
   SPL> index=main server_ip=10.2.1.33
   ```

2. Expand the first event by clicking on the information field as seen in this screenshot:

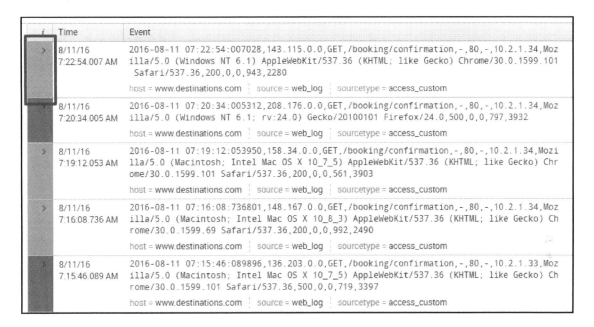

3. While expanded, look for the **server_ip** field. Click on the **Actions** dropdown and select **Edit Tags**:

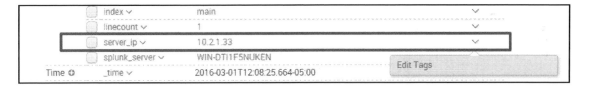

4. In the **Create Tags** window, fill in the **Tag(s)** text area using the following screenshot as a guide. For 10.2.1.33, you will use the following tags: main, patched, east.

5. Click on **Save** when you're done:

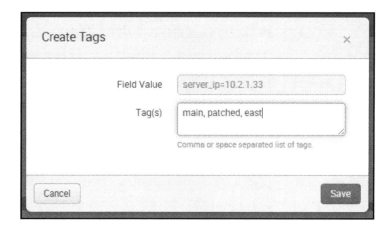

6. Do the same for the remaining two IP addresses and create tags based on the previous table.
7. Now let us make use of this newly-normalized data. Run the search command:

```
SPL> index=main tag=patched OR tag=east
```

This will give you all the events that come from the servers that are patched and hypothetically located in the east side of a building. You can then combine these with other search commands or an event type to narrow down the search results.

Consider a scenario where you need to find all booking payments with errors originating from the servers in the east side of a hypothetical building.

Without event types or tags, you would create a search command that looked something like this:

```
SPL> index=main server_ip=10.2.1.33 OR server_ip=10.2.1.35
     AND (http_uri=/booking/payment http_status_code=500)
```

Compare that to this much more elegant and shorter search command, which you can try
now:

```
SPL> index=main eventtype=bad_payment tag=east
```

Here's an additional exercise for you. Create tags for the following fields using this table as
a guide and use them in a search query:

Fields	Tags
http_uri = /destination/LAX/details	major_destination
http_uri = /destination/NY/details	major_destination
http_uri = /destination/MIA/details	home
http_status_code = 301	redirect
http_status_code = 404	not_found

Now you can use these tags to search for bookings to major destinations, which have a
status code of not_found. These tags can make your searches much easier and more useful.
Here is an example of a search command that combines what you have learned in this
chapter so far:

1. Go ahead and run this now:

   ```
   SPL> eventtype=destination_details tag=major_destination
        tag=not_found
   ```

2. Look through your results and see that you now have data from the destinations
   LAX, NY, and MIA.

Data enrichment with lookups

Occasionally you will come across pieces of data that you wish were rendered in a more
readable manner. A common example is HTTP status codes. Computer engineers are often
familiar with status codes as three-digit numbers. Business analysts, however, would not
necessarily know the meaning of these codes. In Splunk, you solve this predicament by
using lookup tables, which can pair numbers or acronyms with more understandable text
classifiers.

A lookup table is a mapping of keys and values that Splunk can query so it can translate fields into more meaningful information at search time. This is best understood through an example. You can go through the following steps:

1. From the Destinations app, click on**Settings** and then **Lookups**:

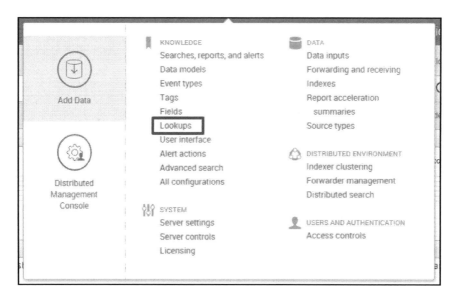

2. In the **Lookups** page, click on the **Add new** option next to **Lookup table files**, as shown in the following screenshot:

3. In the **Add new** page, make sure that the Destinations app is selected.

4. Then, using the following screenshot as your guide, in Upload a lookup file, browse and choose the following: `C:\splunk-essentials\labs\chapter05\http_status.csv`.

5. Finally, type in `http_status.csv` in the **Destination filename** field.

6. Click on **Save** to complete:

The new lookup table file path will now appear in the main **Lookup Table Files** page. Change the permission so that all apps can use it and it will now appear as **Global**. The entries of the lookup table files should be similar to the following screenshot:

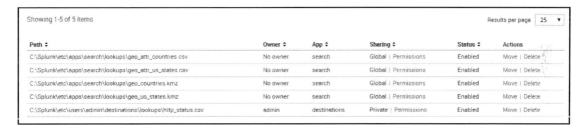

Now that we have configured the lookup table file, it is time to define the lookup:

1. In the **Lookups** page under **Settings**, click on the **Add new** option next to **Lookup definitions**:

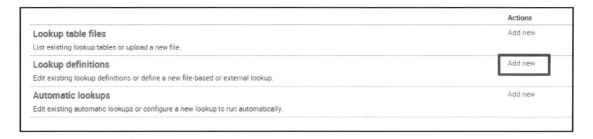

2. Once again, make sure that this is being saved in the context of the Destinations app.
3. In the name field, type in `http_status`.
4. Leave the **Type** as **File-based**. In the **Lookup file** dropdown, look for the `http_status.csv` file and select it.
5. Leave the following checkboxes blank:

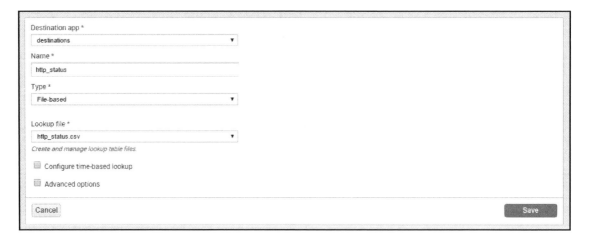

6. Save the definition.
7. The new lookup definition will now appear in the table. Change the permission sharing to **Global** as well.

Let us now try to make use of this new lookup table:

1. In the Destinations app search bar, type in:

```
SPL> eventtype=destination_details | top http_status_code
```

2. The result will show the `http_status_code` column with the raw status codes. Now extend your search by using the `lookup` command. The following multi-line command might not work if you simply copied it. Retyping or re-tabbing is required for it to work:

```
SPL> eventtype=destination_details
                    | top http_status_code
                    | rename http_status_code AS status
                    | lookup http_status status OUTPUT
                      status_description, status_type
```

3. Look at the followi ng output. The steps you took give you a meaningful output showing the description and type of the status codes, all because of the lookup table we first set up:

status	count	percent	status_description	status_type
301	37	21.637427	Moved Permanently	Redirection
200	37	21.637427	OK	Successful
500	36	21.052632	Internal Server Error	Server Error
404	32	18.713450	Not Found	Client Error
302	29	16.959064	Found	Redirection

20 Per Page ∨   Format ∨   Preview ∨

This is good for a first step, but for it to be a practical tool, the lookup needs to happen automatically with all queries. To do this, take the following steps:

1. Go back to **Settings** and then the **Lookups** page.
2. Click on **Add new** to add a new **Automatic Lookup**:

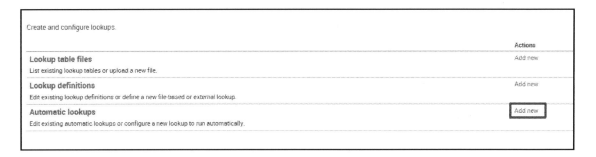

3. Complete the form with the following information. Click on **Save** when you're done. Go to **Permissions** and change the sharing permission to **Global** by clicking on **All Apps**:

Now let's see how these changes can help us out:

1. Go back to the Destinations app search bar and type in the following query.

   `SPL> eventtype=destination_details status_type=Redirection`

> Note that now you can filter your search using the lookup information without invoking the `lookup` command.

2. Notice that the search output will match all events where `http_status_code` equals `301` or `302`.

Creating reports

So far in this chapter, you have learned how to do three very important things: classify data using event types, normalize data using tags, and enrich data using lookup tables. All these, in addition to `Chapter 4`, *Data Models and Pivot*, constitute the essential foundation you need to use Splunk in an efficient manner. Now it is time to put them all to good use.

Splunk reports are reusable searches that can be shared to others or saved as a dashboard. Reports can also be scheduled periodically to perform an action, for example to be sent out as an e-mail. Reports can also be configured to display search results in a statistical table, as well as visualization charts. You can create a report through the search command line or through a Pivot. Here we will create a report using the search command line:

1. In the Destinations app's search page, type in this command:

   `SPL> eventtype=bad_logins | top client_ip`

   The search is trying to find all client IP addresses that attempted to log in but got a 500 internal server error.

2. To save this as a report for future, click on **Save As** | **Report**, then give it the title
   `Bad Logins`:

3. Next, click **Save**.
4. Then click on **View** to go back to the search results.
5. Notice that the report is now properly labeled with our title. You can see the report in the following screenshot:

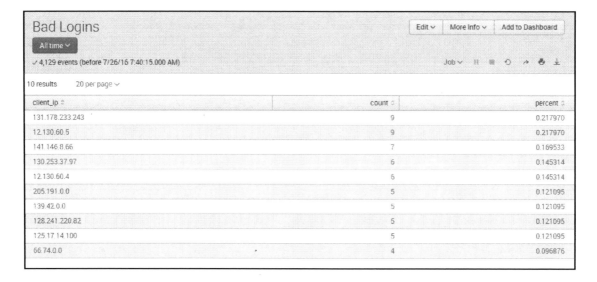

6. If you expand the **Edit** dropdown, you now have additional options to consider while working on this report.

You can modify the permissions so others can use your report. You have done this step a couple of times earlier in the book. This process will be identical to editing permissions for other objects in Splunk.

You can create a schedule to run this report on a timely basis and perform an action on it. The typical action would either be sending the result as an e-mail or running a script. Unfortunately, you would need a mail server to send an e-mail, so you will not be able to do this from your Splunk workstation the way it is currently configured. However, we will show you how it is done:

1. Click **Edit** | **Edit Schedule**.
2. In the pop-up window, click on **Schedule Report**.
3. Change the **Schedule** option to run **Every Day**. The time range applies to the search time scope. The default is to run the report against a 15-minute time range.

   Schedule windows are important for production environments. The schedule window you specify should be less than the time range. When there are multiple concurrent searches going on in the Splunk system, it will check whether you have a schedule window and will delay your report up to the defined time or until no other concurrent searches are running. This is one way of optimizing your Splunk system. If you need accurate results that are based on your time range, however, then do not use the schedule window option.

4. Refer to the following screenshot, then click on **Next** when you're ready to move on:

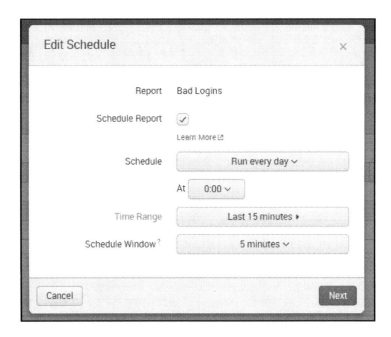

5. In the next window, check the **Send Email** box to show advanced e-mail options. Once again, since your workstation does not have a mail server, the scheduled report will not work. But it is worth viewing what the advanced e-mail options look like:

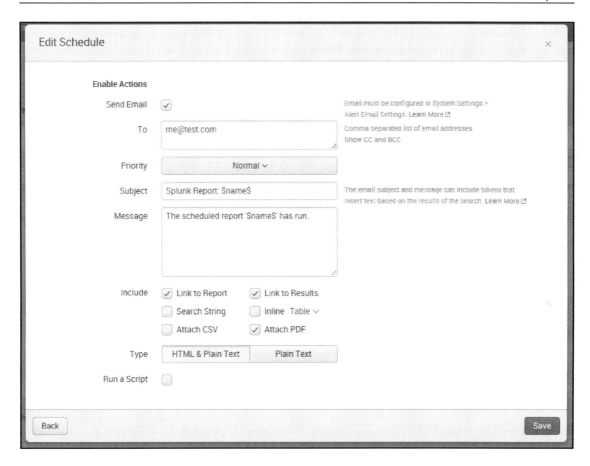

6. Uncheck the **Send Email** option again and click on **Save**. The report will still run, but it will not perform any action. We can, however, embed the report into an external website and it will always show the results based on the scheduled run. We will reserve further discussion about this advanced option for Chapter 7, *Splunk SDK for JavaScript and D3.js*.

There is another option that you will commonly use for reports adding them to dashboards. You can do this with the **Add to Dashboard** button. We will use this option in Chapter 6, *Panes of Glass*.

Create a few more reports from SPL using the following guidelines. We will use some of these reports in future chapters so try your best to do all of them. You can always come back to this chapter if you need to:

Search	Schedule	Report name	Time range	Time window
eventtype="bad_payment" | top client_ip	Run every hour	Bad payments	Last 24 hrs	30 mins
eventtype=good_bookings | timechart span=1h count	Run every 24 hours	Bookings last 24 hrs	Last 24 hrs	15 mins

You also have the ability to create reports using Pivot:

1. Click on **Pivot**.
2. Create a Pivot table on the **Destination Details** child object with **Last 24 hours** as your **Filters** and **Airport Code** as your **Split Rows**.
3. Refer to the following screenshot then save it as a report entitled Destinations by Airport Code. Schedule the report to run every hour, within a 24-hour time range, and with a 30-minute time window:

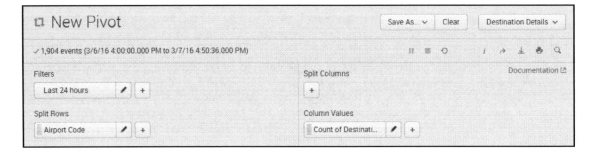

Creating alerts

Alerts are crucial in IT operations. They provide real-time awareness of the state of the systems. Alerts also enable you to act fast when an issue has been detected prior to waiting for a user to report it. Sure enough, you can have a couple of data center operators monitor your dashboards, but nothing jolts their vigil more than an informative alert.

Now, alerts are only good if they are controlled and if they provide enough actionable information. Splunk allows you to do just that. In this section, we will walk you through how to create an actionable alert and how to throttle the alerting to avoid flooding your mailbox.

The exercises in this section will show you how to create an alert, but in order to generate the actual e-mail alert, you will need a mail server. This book will not cover mail servers but the process of creating the alert will be shown in full detail.

We want to know when there are instances of a failed booking scenario. This event type was constructed with the 500 HTTP status code. 5xx status codes are the most devastating errors in a web application so we want to be aware of them. We will now create an alert that will be triggered when a *bad booking* event is detected. Follow these steps:

1. To create the alert, start by typing this:

   ```
   SPL> eventtype=bad_bookings
   ```

2. Click on **Save As | Alert**. In the **Save As Alert** panel, fill up the form using the following screenshot as a guide:

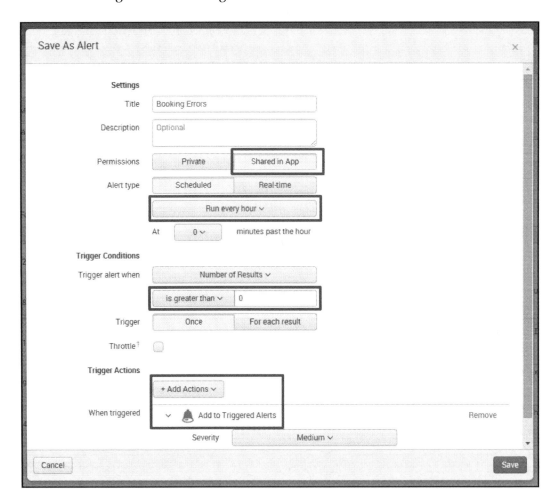

Let us explain some of the different options in this selection:

- **Permissions**: You should be fairly familiar with permissions by now. These apply to alerts as well.
- **Alert type**: There are two ways to create an alert, just as there are two ways to run a search: scheduled (ad hoc) or in real time. Splunk has predefined schedules that you can easily use, namely:
  - Run every hour
  - Run every day

- Run every week
- Run every month
- Although the schedules above are convenient, you will likely soon find yourself wanting more granularity for your searches. This is where the fifth option comes in: **Run on Cron** schedule. We will discuss this in detail later in the chapter.

- **Trigger Conditions**: These are the conditions or rules that define when the alert will be generated. The predefined conditions that Splunk offers out-of-the-box are:
  - **Number of Results**: Most commonly used, this tells the alert to run whenever your search returns a certain number of events.
  - **Number of Hosts**: This is used when you need to know how many hosts are returning events based on your search.
  - **Number of Sources**: This is used when you need to know how many data sources are returning events based on your search.
  - **Custom**: This is used when you want to base your condition on the value of a particular field that is returned in your search result. We will discuss this in detail further into this chapter.

- **Trigger Actions**: These are the actions that will be invoked when your trigger conditions are met. There are several possible default trigger actions currently included in Splunk Enterprise:
  - **Add to Triggered Alerts**: This will add an entry to the **Activity | Triggered alerts** page. This is what we will use in this book since it is the only readily available option.
  - **Run a script**: You can run a script (such as a Python script) located in the `$SPLUNK_HOME/bin/scripts` directory whenever this alert is generated. This is useful for self-repairing issues.
  - **Send e-mail**: Commonly used but requires a mail server to be configured.
  - **Webhook**: A recently introduced type of trigger that allows Splunk to make an HTTP `POST` to an external application (such as Twitter or Slack).

Click on **Save** to save your first alert. We will come back later to optimize it. Meanwhile, you should have now been sent to the alert summary page where you can continue to make changes. Note that since we selected the **Add to Triggered Alerts** action, you should now see the history of when this alert was triggered on your machine. Since the Eventgen data is randomized and we scheduled it to run every hour, you may have to wait until the next hour for results:

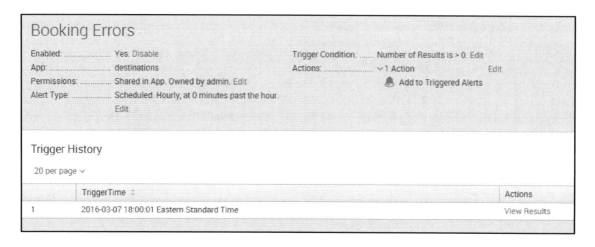

Search and report acceleration

In Chapter 4, *Data Models and Pivot,* you learned how to accelerate a data model to speed up retrieval of data. The same principle applies to saved searches or reports:

1. Click on the **Reports** link in the navigation menu of the Destinations app.
2. Click on the **Edit | Edit Acceleration** option in the **Bookings Last 24 Hrs** report.
3. Enable **1 Day** acceleration as seen in the following screenshot:

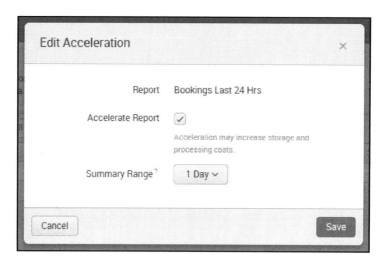

4. To check the progress of your report's acceleration, click on **Settings** | **Report Acceleration Summaries**:

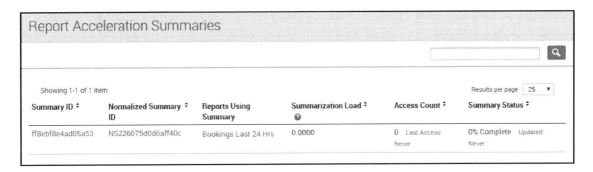

Scheduling best practices

No matter how advanced and well-scaled your Splunk infrastructure is, if all scheduled searches and reports are running at the same time, the system will start experiencing issues. Typically you will receive a Splunk message saying that you have reached the limit of concurrent or historical searches. Suffice to say that there are only a certain number of searches that can be run on CPU core for each Splunk instance. The very first issue a beginner Splunk admin faces is how to limit the number of concurrent searches running at the same time. One way to fix this is to throw more servers into the Splunk cluster, but that is not the efficient way.

The trick to establishing a robust system is to properly stagger and budget scheduled searches and reports. This means ensuring that they are not running at the same time. There are two ways to achieve this:

- **Time windows**: The first way to ensure that searches are not running concurrently is to always set a time window. You have done this in the exercises in this chapter. This is not ideal if you need to schedule runs so that the schedule of each run always happen at an exact time.
- **Custom Cron schedule**: This is what most advanced users use to create their schedules. Cron is a system daemon, or a computer program that runs as a background process, derived from traditional UNIX systems; it is used to execute tasks at specified times.

Let us see an example of how to use a custom Cron schedule. Begin with this search query, which finds all errors in a payment:

1. Type in the following:

   SPL> eventtype=bad_payment

2. Save it as an alert by clicking on **Save As | Alert**.
3. Name it Payment Errors.
4. Change the permissions to Shared in App.
5. In the **Alert type**, change the schedule to **Run on Cron Schedule**.
6. In the **Earliest** field, enter −15m@m (last 15 minutes and snap at the beginning of the minute. This means a time range of 15 minutes and also ensures that it starts at the beginning of that minute).
7. In the **Latest** field, type in now. In the **Cron Expression** field, type in */5 * * * *.
8. Finally, change the **Trigger Actions** to **Add to Triggered Alerts**. Use the following screenshot as a guide:

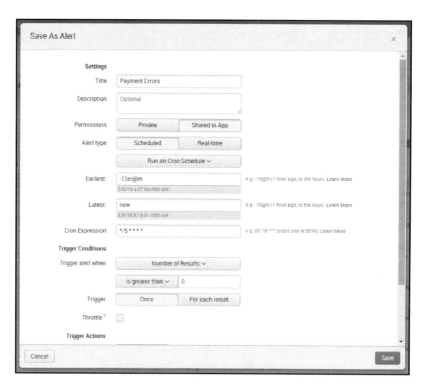

9. Click **Save** when done.

The Cron expression * * * * * corresponds to minute hour day month day-of-week.

Learning Cron expressions is easiest when you look at examples. The more examples, the simpler it is to understand this method of scheduling. Here are some typical examples:

Cron expression	Schedule
*/5 * * * *	Every 5 minutes
*/15 * * * *	Every 15 minutes
0 */6 * * *	Every 6 hours, on the hour
30 */2 * * *	Every 2 hours at the 30th minute (for instance, 3:30)
45 14 1,10 * *	Every 1st and 10th of the month, at 2:45 pm.
0 */1 * 1-5	Every hour, Monday to Friday
2,17,32,47 * * * *	Every 2nd minute, 17th minute, 32nd minute, and 47th minute of every hour.

Now that you know something about Cron expressions, you can fine-tune all your searches to run in precise and different schedules.

Summary indexing

In a matter of days, Splunk will accumulate data and start to move events into the cold bucket. If you recall, the cold bucket is where data is stored to disk. You will still be able to access this data but you are bound by the speed of the disk. Compound that with the millions of events that are typical with an enterprise Splunk implementation, and you can understand how your historical searches can slow down at an exponential rate.

There are two ways to circumvent this problem, one of which you have already performed: search acceleration and summary indexing.

With summary indexing, you run a scheduled search and output the results into an index called summary. The result will only show the computed statistics of the search. This results in a very small subset of data that will seemingly be faster to retrieve than going through the entirety of the events in the cold bucket.

Say, for example, you wish to keep track of all counts of an error in payment and you wish to keep the data in the summary index. Follow these steps:

1. From your Destinations app, go to **Settings** | **Searches**, reports, and alerts.
2. Click on the **New** button to create a new scheduled search.
3. Use the following information as a guide:
   - **Destinations app**: Destinations
   - **Search name**: Summary of Payment Errors
   - **Search**: eventtype=bad_payment | stats count
   - **Start time**: -2m@m
   - **Finish time**: now

Now perform the following steps:

1. Click on **Schedule this search**.
2. Change **Schedule type** to **Cron**.

3. Set **Cron schedule** to */2 * * * *.
4. Set **Condition** to **always**. This option, present in the **Alert** section denotes if the number of events is greater than 0.
5. Set **Expiration** to **Custom time** of 1 hour.

Use the following screenshot as a guide:

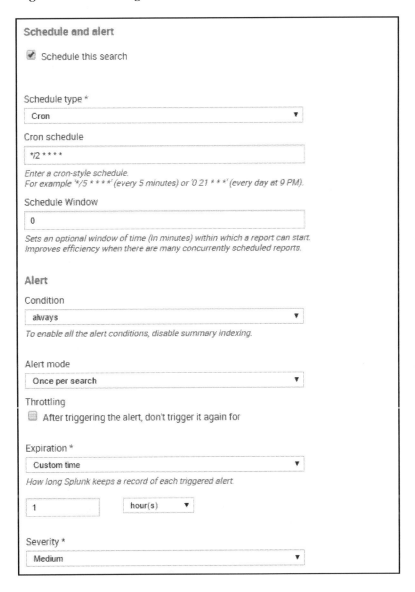

Now perform the following steps:

1. Click on the **Enable** checkbox in the **Summary indexing** section
2. Add a new field in the **Add fields** section, where values will be `summaryCount` equals to `count`

Use the following information as a guide:

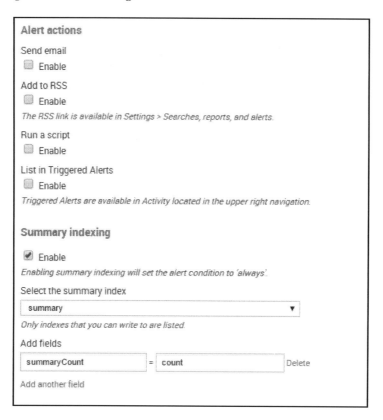

1. Save when you are ready to continue.
2. Now go back to the Destinations app's **Search** page. Type in the following search command and wait about 5-10 minutes:

```
SPL> index=summary search_name="Summary of Payment Errors"
```

Notice that this stripped the original event of all other information except the count of events at the time that the scheduled search is running. We will use this information in later chapters to create optimized dashboards.

Summary

In this chapter, you have learned how to optimize data in three ways: classifying your data using event types, normalizing your data using tags, and enriching your data using lookup tables. You have also learned how to create advanced reports and alerts. You have accelerated your searches just like you did with data models. You have been introduced to the powerful Cron expression, which allows you to create granularity on your scheduled searches, and you have also been shown how to stagger your searches using time windows. Finally, you have created a summary index that allows you to search historical data faster. In the next chapter, Chapter 6, *Panes of Glass*, you will go on to learn more about how to do visualizations.

6
Panes of Glass

Splunk makes it easy to visualize data, and in this chapter we will show how to do that through a *pane of glass* or what is sometimes called a *single pane of glass* dashboard. This just means a dashboard that is designed with an effective graphic user interface that is easy to navigate and carefully laid out to be useful. This ability to make dashboards is one of Splunk's most useful features. Most of the charts that you will need to represent your data are already built into the application and you can organize these with very minimal effort. With practice, you can spin off a dashboard in a fraction of the time you might expect it to take.

In this chapter, we will work on the following topics:

- How to identify the different types of dashboard
- How to gather business requirements
- How to modify dashboard panels
- Building a single pane of glass dashboard with key performance indicators

Creating effective dashboards

It is easy to use Splunk to develop an attractive dashboard with multiple panels. However, this is not usually the best way to present your information. This is because a dashboard with multiple panels generally requires scrolling down the page, which can take the viewer's eyes away from crucial information. An effective dashboard should generally meet the following conditions:

- **Single page**: The dashboard fits on a single page with no scrolling required
- **Multiple data points displayed**: Charts and visualizations should display a number of data points

- **Crucial information highlighted**: The dashboard points out the most important information, using appropriate titles, labels, legends, and markers
- **Created with the user in mind**: Data is summarized in a way that is meaningful to the viewer

- **Loads quickly**: The dashboard loads in a few seconds
- **Avoid redundancy**: The display does not repeat information in multiple places

Types of dashboard

There are three kinds of dashboard that you will typically create with Splunk:

- Dynamic form-based dashboards
- Static real-time dashboards
- Dashboards as scheduled reports

Dynamic form-based dashboards allow Splunk users to change the dashboard data without leaving the page. This is accomplished by adding input fields (such as time, radio (button), textbox, checkbox, dropdown, and so on) in the dashboard, which changes the data based on the current selection. This is an effective type of dashboard for teams that troubleshoot issues and analyze data.

Static real-time dashboards are often kept on a big panel screen for constant viewing, simply because they are so useful. You see these dashboards in data centers or **Network Operations Centers (NOCs)**. Even though they are called **static**, in fact the data changes in real time without refreshing the page; it is just the format that stays constant. The dashboard will also have indicators and alerts that allow operators to easily identify a problem and act on it. Dashboards like this usually show the current state of the network or business systems, using indicators for web performance and traffic, revenue flow, and other important measures.

Dashboards as scheduled reports are the only kind that breaks away from the rules mentioned previously. This type will typically have multiple panels included on the same page. Also, the dashboard will not be exposed for viewing; it will generally be saved as a PDF file and sent to e-mail recipients at scheduled times. This format is ideal when you need to send information updates to multiple recipients at regular intervals.

In this chapter, we will create these three types of dashboard. You will also learn how to use and interact with the Splunk Dashboard Editor to develop advanced visualizations.

Gathering information and business requirements

Since you have signed in to the Splunk system with the user name `Admin`, you are considered a Splunk admin. With this exalted position come duties, one of which is being responsible for the data. As a custodian of data, a Splunk admin has a free rein over how to interpret and present the information to users. It is common that the administrator will be the one to create the first few dashboards. A more mature implementation, however, requires collaboration between different groups to create an output that is beneficial to all.

As a Splunk admin, make it a habit to consistently request feedback from your users regarding the dashboards. Without feedback, the dashboard that you created will only reflect your ideas and desires, not those of the rest of the team, whoever they may be. Sit down with the day-to-day users and lay out, on a drawing board, the business flow or the system diagrams to understand how things really work. Ask for users' stream-of-consciousness thoughts as you observe them use the dashboard in their work. Interview them and ask what data matters to them. Look for key phrases like these, which signify what data is most important to the business:

- *If this is broken, we lose tons of revenue...*
- *This is an operations bottleneck and a constant point of failure...*
- *We don't know what's going on here...*
- *If only I can see the trend, it will make my work easier...*
- *This is what my boss wants to see...*

The people who will use your dashboard come from many areas of the business. You want to talk to all the different users, no matter where they are on the organizational chart. When you make friends with the architects, developers, business analysts, and management, you will end up building dashboards that benefit the entire organization.

We hope at this point that you have been convinced of the importance of dashboards and are ready to get started creating some, as we will do in the following sections.

Dynamic form-based dashboard

In this section, we will create a dynamic form-based dashboard in our Destinations app that will allow users to interact with form inputs to change and redisplay the data. Here is a screenshot of the final output of this dynamic form-based dashboard:

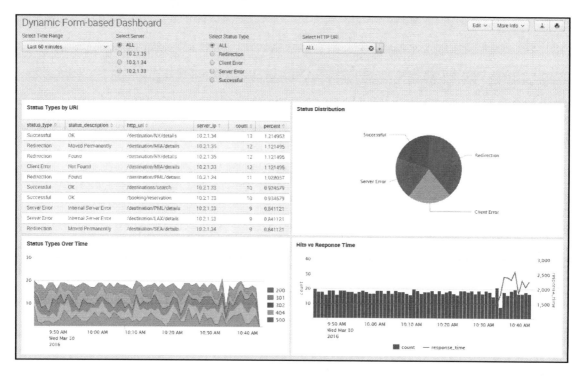

Dynamic dashboard with form input

Let's begin by creating the dashboard itself and then generating the base panels:

1. Open the Destinations app.
2. Run this search command:

```
SPL> index=main status_type="*" http_uri="*" server_ip="*"
     | top status_type, status_description, http_uri, server_ip
```

Important

Be careful when copying commands with quotation marks. It is best to type in the entire search command to avoid problems.

3. Click on **Save As | Dashboard Panel**.

4. Fill in the information based on the following screenshot:

5. Click on **Save**.

6. Close the pop-up window that appears.

Creating a Status Distribution panel

We will go to the dashboard later, once all our panel searches have been generated. Let us go ahead and create the second panel:

1. In the search window, type in the following search command:

   ```
   SPL> index=main status_type="*" http_uri=* server_ip=*
        | top status_type
   ```

2. You will save this as a dashboard panel to the newly-created dashboard. In the **Dashboard** option, click on the **Existing** button and look for the new dashboard, as seen here. Don't forget to fill in the **Panel Title** as **Status Distribution**:

3. Click on **Save** when you are done.

Creating the Status Types Over Time panel

Now we'll move on to create the next panel:

1. Type in the following search command:

```
SPL> index=main status_type="*" http_uri=* server_ip=*
     | timechart count by http_status_code
```

2. You will save this as a `Dynamic Form-based Dashboard` panel as well. Type in `Status Types Over Time` in the **Panel Title** field:

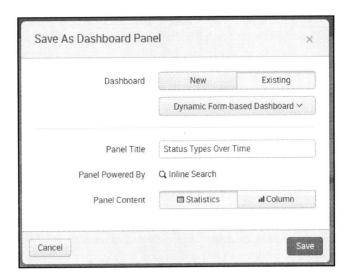

3. Click on **Save**.

Creating the Hits vs Response Time panel

Now on to the next panel. Use the following search command:

```
SPL> index=main status_type="*" http_uri=* server_ip=*
     | timechart count, avg(http_response_time) as response_time
```

Save this dashboard panel as Hits vs Response Time:

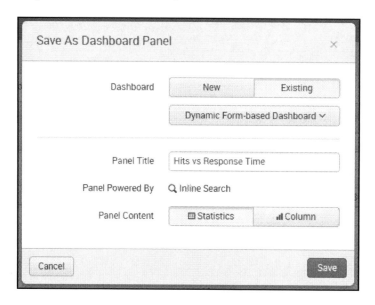

Arranging the dashboard

Now, we'll go on to look at the dashboard we've created and make a few changes.

1. Click on the **View Dashboard** button. If you missed out on the **View Dashboard** button, you can find your dashboard by clicking on **Dashboards** in the main navigation bar.
2. Let us edit the panel arrangement. Click on **Edit | Edit Panels**.
3. Move the **Status Distribution** panel to the upper-right row.
4. Move the **Hits vs Response Time** panel to the lower-right row.
5. Click on **Done** to save your layout changes.

Look at the following screenshot. The dashboard framework you've created should now look much like this.

The dashboard probably looks a little plainer than you expected it to. But don't worry about how it looks for now. We will fix the dashboard one panel at a time.

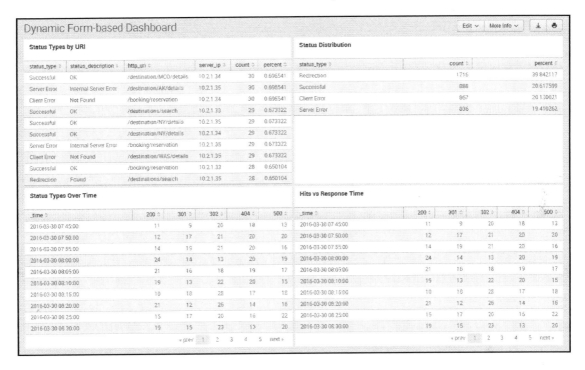

Dynamic dashboard with four panels in tabular formats

Now that we have the layout framework in place, let us start modifying the panels. The first panel is how we want it to look so we do not need to change it.

Panel options

In this section, we will learn how to alter the look of our panels and create visualizations in them.

Go to Edit mode by clicking on **Edit** | **Edit Panels**.

Each dashboard panel will have three setting options to work with: inline search options, visualization type, and visualization options. They are represented by three dropdown icons.

The **INLINE SEARCH** drop-down allows you to modify the title, change the search string, change the time modifier for the search string, convert the panel into a report, and delete the panel.

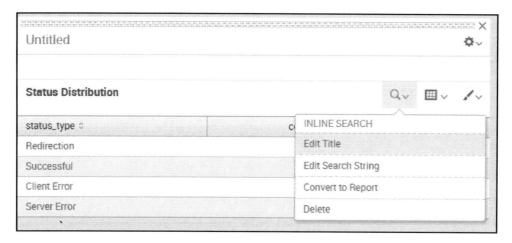

The **Visualization Type** drop-down allows you to change the type of visualization to use for the panel, as shown in the following screenshot:

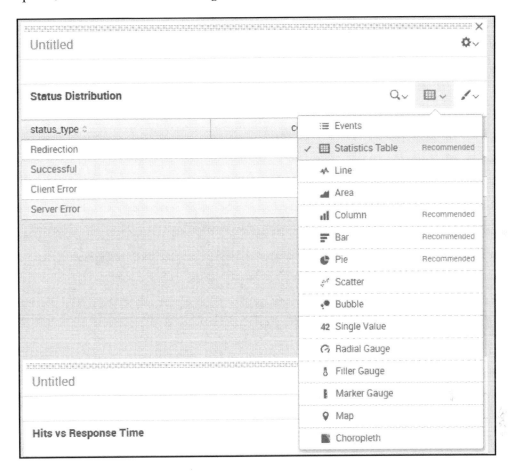

Finally, the **Visualization Options** drop-down will give you the ability to fine-tune your visualization. These options will change depending on the visualization you select. For a normal statistics table, this is how it will look.

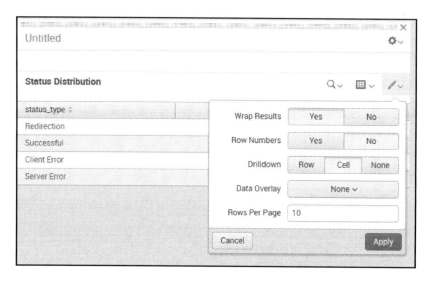

Pie chart – status distribution

Go ahead and change the **Status Distribution** visualization panel to a pie chart. You do this by selecting the **Visualization Type** dropdown and selecting **Pie**. Once done, the panel will look like the following screenshot:

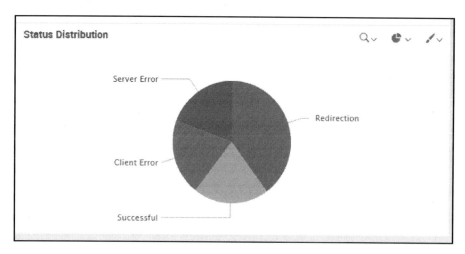

Stacked area chart – Status Types Over Time

Change the **Status Types Over Time** panel to **Area**. By default, area charts will not be stacked. Let us fix this by clicking on the **Visualization Options** dropdown.

1. In the **Stack Mode** section, click on **Stacked**. For **Null Values**, select **Zero**. Use the chart that follows for guidance.

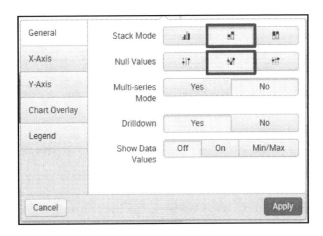

2. Click on **Apply**. The panel will change right away.
3. Let us clean it up further. Let us remove the _time label as it is already implied. You can do this in the **X-Axis** section by setting the **Title** to **None**.

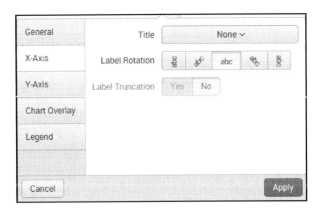

Here now is the new stacked area chart panel.

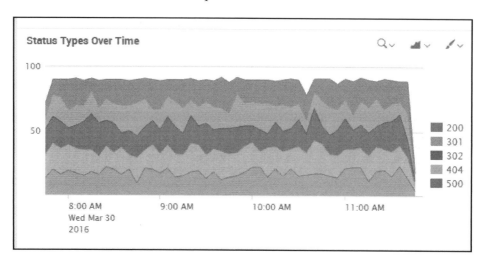

Column with line overlay combo chart – Hits vs Response Time

Now we are going to create a chart that combines a column and a line for the **Hits vs. Response Time** panel. This is good to use when representing two or more kinds of data with different ranges.

1. First change the chart panel visualization to **Column**.
2. In the **Visualization Options** dropdown, click on **Chart Overlay**.
3. In the **Overlay** selection box, select **response_time**.
4. Turn on **View as Axis** and click **X-Axis**.
5. Change **Title** to **None**.
6. Click on **Legend**.
7. Change the **Legend Position** to **Bottom**.
8. Click on **Apply**.

The new panel will now look similar to the following screenshot. Our data is not fluctuating much but imagine this with real data and you can easily spot trends and anomalies within the same time frame.

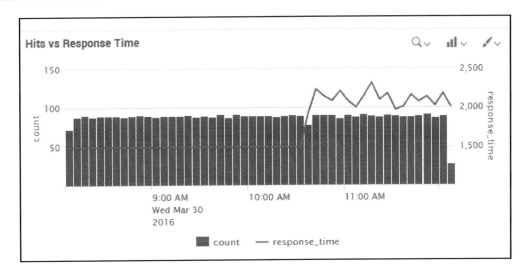

9. Click on **Done** to save all the changes you made and exit the **Edit** mode.

The dashboard has now come to life. This is how it should look now.

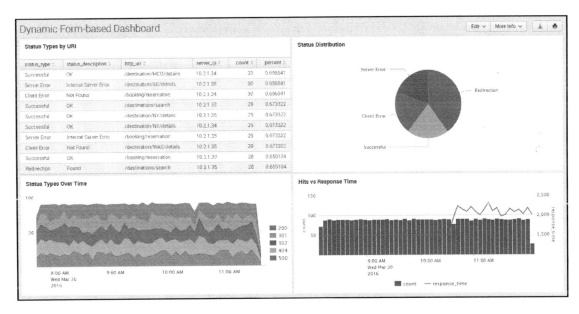

Dynamic form-based dashboard with four panels in different formats

Form inputs

Now that we have the dashboard layout that we want, it is time to make it dynamic and interactive. Before we proceed, let us just highlight some of the basic key concepts related to form inputs.

Just as in any web page, a form input is an element that allows you to select or type in information that will be submitted to the application for processing. There are different form inputs available for Splunk dashboards:

- Text
- Radio (which uses a radio button)
- Dropdown (which uses a dropdown menu or list)
- Checkbox
- Multiselect (which allows you to select several responses)
- Link list (this is a horizontal list that contains clickable links)
- Time
- Submit

If you click on **Edit | Edit Panels**, you will see that you can select which **Form Input** you require by clicking on the **Add Input** dropdown.

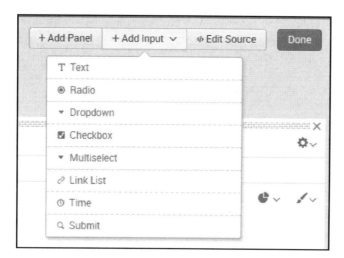

1. Go ahead and select **Text** in the **Add Input** drop-down. A new editable input field panel will be added at the very top of the dashboard. You can either edit the properties of the field using the pencil icon or delete the field entirely using the **x** icon.

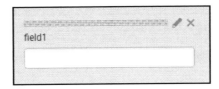

2. Click on the pencil icon to edit the properties. You can change the type of input by clicking on the selections on the left of the pop-up window.

Although the options are generally different for every type of input, there are common concepts that you need to fully comprehend. So it is worth looking at this list carefully before we take you through some examples.

In the **General** section, you'll see the following options:

- **Label**: Every input needs a label. This is what will be shown on the dashboard as the title of the input. An example of this would be: **Select Sourcetype**.
- **Search on Change**: If checked, this checkbox triggers a reload of all panels that depend on the specific input. You typically want this checked, and want to be sure to include it if you think that the input will likely change.

In the **Token Options** section, you'll see the following option:

- **Token**: This is an identifier for the field. It is used to associate the value that is returned by the form input against the identifier or token name. In programming, this is what you would refer to as a variable or ID. For example, if you created an input for time and you named the token `time1`, then in your panel's search query you can extract the value of the input field by calling the identifier `$time1$`. Then the tokens that we use to get specific fields will be `$time1$.earliest` and `$time1$.latest`. You will walk through other examples in this chapter.
- **Default**: On inputs that require a selection, you can specify a default value during page load. This is important if your panel charts require an initial value to populate the data. If not, your panels will not load data until the user selects an option.

In the **Static Options** section, you'll see the following option:

- **Name and Value**: These are name-value pairs that will appear in the selection of the input field. For example, in a dropdown, if you have added a name called *foo* with the value *bar*, then *foo* will appear in the dropdown list but the value behind it is *bar*.

In the **Dynamic Options** section, you'll see the following options:

- **Search String**: Occasionally the selection that you need shown in the input fields is already in Splunk. With this option, you can use a search query to populate the input field dynamically. For example, the search query `index=main | top host` will allow the input field to show all top hosts as a selectable option.
- **Time Range**: This is the time range for the search query used previously. Try to use a small time range here.

- **Field for Label**: This is the field that returns the value you need based on the search string. In the example previously, you need the field *host*.
- **Field for Value**: You can change the field for the value but we recommend you use the same one as the label.

Creating a time range input

Let us change our input field into a time range field.

1. Click on **Add Input**.
2. On the list to the left, select **Time**.
3. In the **General** section, type **Select Time Range** in the **Label** space.
4. Click on the **Search on Change** checkbox.
5. Set the **Default** time range to Last 24 Hours.
6. Use the following screenshot as a guide.
7. Click Apply when done:

8. Before you save the dashboard changes, click the **Autorun dashboard** checkbox, as seen in the following screenshot:

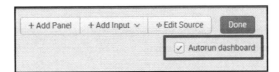

You can now try to change the time range using the time input, but nothing will happen. This is because we have not yet configured the panels to react when the time input has been changed. Let us do that now:

1. Go back to **Edit | Edit Panels** mode.
2. Select **Inline Search** and edit **Search String** on the first panel.
3. Change **Time Range Scope** to **Shared Time Picker (time)**.
4. Click on **Save**:

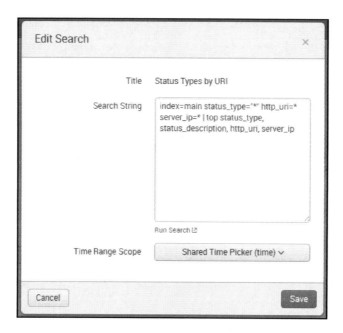

Notice that the data on the first panel now reacts to the changes you make on the time range input. Perform the same steps on the other three panels and watch the data change based on your selected time range.

Creating a radio input

Now we are going to create radio inputs with dynamic search options. This will allow viewers to select server and status types, and will affect the information rendered by the panels:

1. Click on **Edit** | **Edit Panels**.
2. Select **Add Input** | **Radio**.
3. Click on the **Edit** icon in the newly created input.
4. In the **Label** field, type in `Select Server`.
5. Enable **Search on Change** by checking the checkbox.
6. In the **Token** field, type `server`:

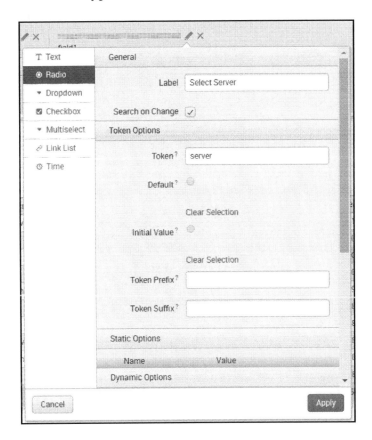

7. Scroll down to **Static Options** and click on it. In **Static Options**, add **Name** as
   ALL and **Value** as *.

8. Click **Dynamic Options**, then fill in **Search String**, entering the following search
   command:

   ```
   SPL> index=main | top server_ip
   ```

9. Change the time range from **All time** to **Last 60 minutes**.

10. In **Field For Label**, type in server_ip.

11. In **Field For Value**, type in server_ip.

12. Now scroll back up to **Token Options**.

13. For **Default**, select **ALL**.

14. For **Initial Value**, select **ALL**.

15. Click **Apply** and you're done:

Now that you have configured the radio input with dynamic search options, you will see that the selection has been populated, along with the static option that you created. This is a great way of creating selection inputs when you know that the items will regularly change depending on a search query:

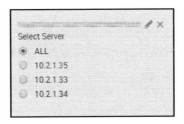

Try this exercise to reinforce what you have learned. Create a second radio input option, following the same steps as previously, with the following information:

- **Label**: Select Status Type
- **Search on Change**: Check
- **Token**: status_type
- **Static Options**: { Name: ALL, Value: * }
- **Search String**: index=main | top status_type
- **Time Range**: Last 60 minutes
- **Field For Label**: status_type
- **Field For Value**: status_type
- **Token Options Default**: ALL
- **Token Options Initial Value**: ALL

Click on **Apply** to save your changes.

If you did it correctly, the newly-created radio input will look like this:

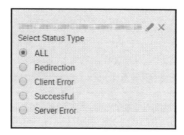

Similar to when we first created the **Time** input, the panels will not react to these new inputs until we associate them. In order for the new inputs to change the values in the panels, we have to modify each panel search string to include the new tokens server and status_type:

1. For the **Status Types by URI** panel, click on the **Inline Search** dropdown.
2. Select **Edit Search String**.
3. Carefully change the search string to match the following highlighted changes. This will filter the search results to show information for selected status_type and server_ip:

```
SPL> index=main status_type="$status_type$"
     http_uri=* server_ip=$server$
     | top status_type, status_description, http_uri, server_ip
```

4. Click on **Save**.
5. Then click on **Apply** to save the changes to the form input.
6. Click on **Done** to exit out of **Edit** mode.
7. Refresh the entire page using your browser's refresh icon.
8. Now change the selections of both the **Select Server** input and the **Select Status Type** input, and make sure the data on the first panel is changing.

Here is an example of data being filtered to **10.2.1.34** and **Redirection** for data arriving in the last 60 minutes:

Select Time Range	Select Server	Select Status Type
Last 60 minutes ⌄	○ ALL ○ 10.2.1.35 ● 10.2.1.34 ○ 10.2.1.33	○ ALL ● Redirection ○ Successful ○ Client Error ○ Server Error

Status Types by URI

status_type ⇅	status_description ⇅	http_uri ⇅	server_ip ⇅	count ⇅	percent ⇅
Redirection	Moved Permanently	/home	10.2.1.34	9	5.921053
Redirection	Found	/booking/payment	10.2.1.34	9	5.921053
Redirection	Found	/destination/WAS/details	10.2.1.34	8	5.263158
Redirection	Moved Permanently	/destination/WAS/details	10.2.1.34	7	4.605263
Redirection	Moved Permanently	/auth	10.2.1.34	7	4.605263
Redirection	Found	/destination/MIA/details	10.2.1.34	7	4.605263
Redirection	Found	/booking/confirmation	10.2.1.34	7	4.605263
Redirection	Moved Permanently	/destinations/search	10.2.1.34	6	3.947368
Redirection	Moved Permanently	/destination/MIA/details	10.2.1.34	6	3.947368
Redirection	Found	/destination/PML/details	10.2.1.34	6	3.947368

At this point, you will appreciate what form input does to your dashboard. By simply substituting tokens in your search string, you are dynamically altering the panel charts so your users can filter the data in the ways they need. Continue editing the remaining panels using the following guide. You can refresh your browser if the changes do not happen right away.

1. Edit the **Status Distribution** panel to show the top ten status types:

```
SPL> index=main status_type="$status_type$"
     http_uri=* server_ip=$server$
     | top status_type
```

2. Edit the **Status Over Time** panel to show a timechart with counts reflecting status codes:

```
SPL> index=main status_type="$status_type$"
     http_uri=* server_ip=$server$
     | timechart count by http_status_code
```

3. Edit the **Hits vs Response Time** panel to show a timechart with counts for the number of events at each time and the average values for `http_response_time` for each time category (chosen by default, depending on the time span), labeled as `response_time`:

```
SPL> index=main status_type="$status_type$"
     http_uri=* server_ip=$server$
     | timechart count, avg(http_response_time) as response_time
```

Creating a dropdown input

Dropdown inputs function exactly the same as radio inputs. The former is used when the selection is huge and you do not want the list of choices to unnecessarily clutter the entire page. The `http_uri` field has numerous results, so this makes a drop-down the ideal candidate for input here.

Follow the same procedure as for radio input creation, but make sure you have selected **Dropdown** instead. Use the following information and screenshots as guides to complete the task:

1. Click on **Edit | Edit Panels**.
2. Select **Add Input | Dropdown**.
3. Click the **Edit** icon in the newly created input.
4. In the **Label** field, type in `Select HTTP URI` to name your new drop-down.
5. As you did when you created a radio button, enable **Search on Change** by checking the checkbox.
6. In the **Token** field, type `http_uri`.
7. Under **Token Options** section, in **Default**, select `ALL`.
8. Under **Token Options** section, in **Initial Value**, select `ALL`.
9. For **Static Options**, type `{ Name: ALL, Value: * }`.
10. Under **Dynamic Options**, be sure the search icon is selected.

11. In the search string, type the following to designate that you want the index labeled main and top 0 to designate that you want to return all values of `http_uri`:

    SPL> index=main | top 0 http_uri

12. For the time range, specify **Last 60 minutes**.
13. In **Field** for **Label**, type `http_uri`.
14. In the **Field** for **Value**, also `designatehttp_uri`.
15. Click on **Apply** to save your changes:

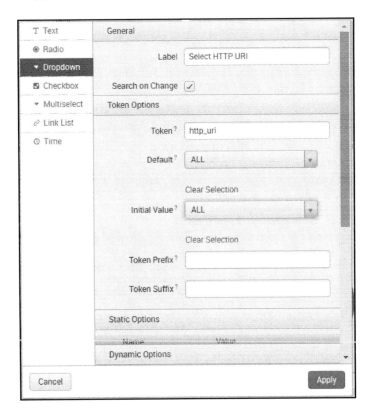

If done correctly, the newly-created drop-down input will look like this:

Now that you have created the inputs, go ahead and associate them with the search panels. The same procedure applies; you have to edit each search string to include the new token:

1. Add the new dropdown token you have created to the **Status Distribution** panel, which will return the top 10 (by default) status types, along with their status descriptions, http_uri values, and server_ip values: http_uri=$http_uri$

   ```
   SPL> index=main status_type="$status_type$" http_uri=$http_uri$
        server_ip=$server$ | top status_type, status_description,
        http_uri, server_ip
   ```

2. Also add the same token to the **Status Over Time** panel, which will then return a timechart of the top 10 counts for http_status_code:

   ```
   SPL> index=main status_type="$status_type$" http_uri=$http_uri$
        server_ip=$server$ | timechart count by http_status_code
   ```

3. And finally, add the token to the **Hits vs Response Time** panel, which will return a timechart showing the top 10 counts for average values of http_response_time (labeled as response_time):

   ```
   SPL> index=main status_type="$status_type$" http_uri=$http_uri$
        server_ip=$server$ | timechart count, avg(http_response_time) as
        response_time
   ```

When all the form inputs are done, this is how it should look. We show the heading, where you can filter, first:

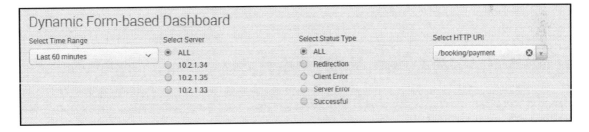

This is now a fully-functional, dynamic, form-based dashboard. It was a lot of work, but the more you do it, the easier the process becomes.

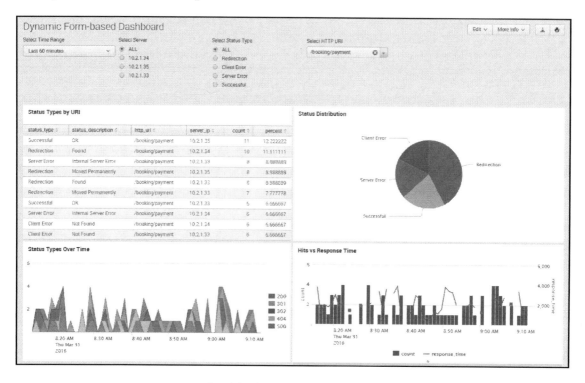

Dynamic form-based dashboard with four chart panels

Static Real-Time dashboard

In this section, we will create a real-time dashboard that will display crucial information based on the data we have. To encourage you, we present a screenshot here with how it will look when we are done:

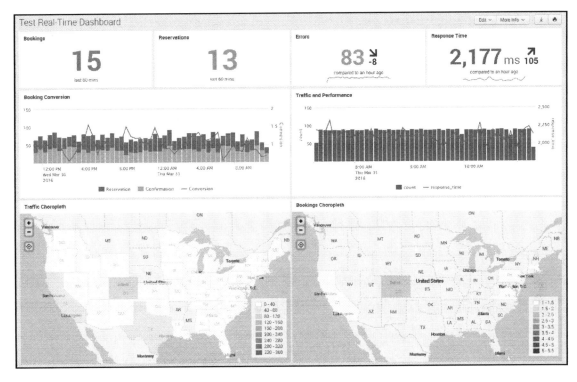

Test real-time dashboard with advanced indicators, combo charts, and choropleth charts

Single Value Panels with color ranges

In the previous sections, you first created panels by running a search then saving them in a dashboard. After you created all your search panels, you then started to modify the visualization from the dashboard. This is one way to achieve it. However, typically you first want to see your visualization before adding it to a dashboard. This makes it a more straightforward approach. We will use that method in upcoming sections:

1. Let's start with a search command in the Destinations app to create the dashboard:

   ```
   SPL> index=main http_uri=/booking/confirmation http_status_code=200
       | stats count
   ```

2. Select **Real-Time > 1 hour window** in the **Time Range** preset and run the command.

3. Click on the **Visualization** tab to switch to visualization mode.

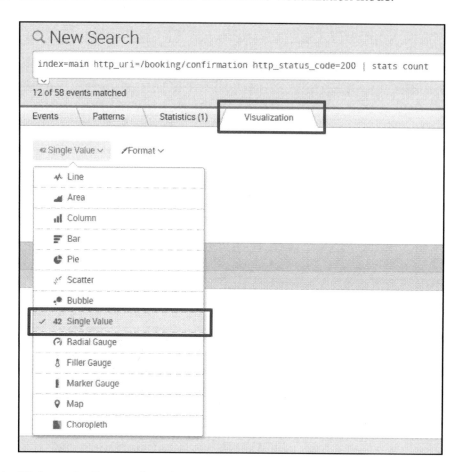

4. Click on the **Format** dropdown.
5. In the **Under Label** field, type last 60 mins.

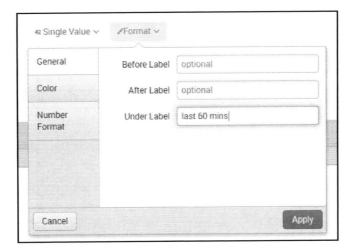

6. In the **Color** tab, click on **Yes** to **Use Colors**.
7. Arrange the color ranges to match the following screenshot:

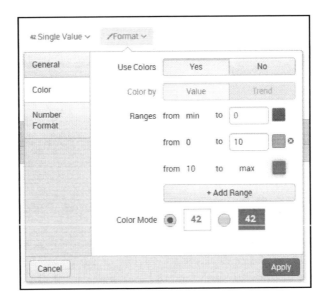

8. Click on **Apply**.
9. Click on **Save As | Dashboard** panel.

10. Select **New dashboard** and fill in the following information:

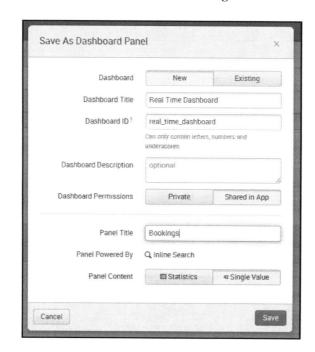

11. Click on **Save**.
12. Click on **View Dashboard**.

The panel you just created is set to **Real Time search** and will continuously update as long as the page is in view and you have not exceeded your real-time search quota.

Creating panels by cloning

There will be multiple occasions when you will need the same visualization for a different set of data. A very cool way of quickly doing this is by cloning previously created panels. We will create another color-coded single value panel by cloning the first one we created:

1. In your **Real Time** dashboard, go to edit mode by clicking on **Edit | Edit Panels**.
2. Click on **Add Panel**. The **Add Panel** slide-through will appear.
3. Expand **Clone from Dashboard**.
4. Expand **Real Time Dashboard**.

5. Click on **Bookings**. Use the following screenshot as a guide:

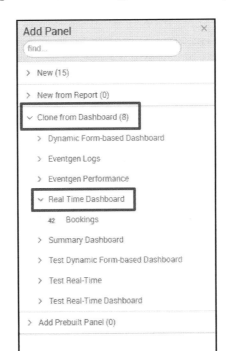

6. In the **Preview** pane, click on **Add to Dashboard**.
7. Click the title of the second **Bookings** panel and rename it `Reservations`.
8. Click on the **Search modification** dropdown and select **Edit Search String**.
9. Change the **Search String** to the following command:

```
SPL> index=main http_uri=/booking/reservation http_status_code=200
     | stats count
```

10. Click on **Save**.
11. Drag the second panel to the right of the first row.
12. Click on **Done** to save your settings.

You have successfully cloned a panel and shortened dashboard creation by a number of steps.

Single Value Panels with trends

We will now create two more single value panels that indicate trend lines. This is useful when you need your viewer to understand the behavior of the data in a very compressed line chart while highlighting the most current value. This is commonly used in viewing financial stock prices:

1. Enter edit mode with **Edit | Edit Panels**.
2. Create a clone of the **Bookings** panel. Follow the steps in the previous section.
3. Add it to the dashboard.
4. Rename the new panel **Errors**.
5. Change the **Search String** to the following command:

   ```
   SPL> index=main http_status_code=5* | timechart count
   ```

6. Click on the **Visualization Options** dropdown.
7. Set **Under Label** to last 60 mins.
8. Click on **Yes** for **Show Trend Indicator**.
9. In the **Compared to** dropdown, select **1 hour before**.
10. Ensure that **Show Sparkline** is set to **Yes**.
11. Refer to the following screenshot:

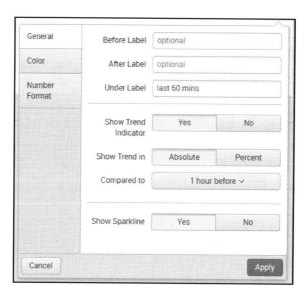

12. Click on **Apply**.
13. Click on the **Search** dropdown | **Edit Search String**.
14. In **Select Time Range**, click **Real-time**.
15. Change the **Earliest** value to **24 Hours Ago**:

16. Click on **Apply**, then **Save**.
17. Drag the panel to the right end of the first row.
18. After following the previous steps, click on the **Done** button.

Repeat the previous procedure to create another panel. Use the following information to build the new panel:

- **Title**: Response Time
- **Search String**: index=main | timechart avg(http_response_time) as response_time span=1h

- **Time Range**: Real-time 24 Hours Ago
- **After Label**: ms
- **Under Label**: compared to an hour ago
- **Show Trend in**: Percent

The new single value panels have been created and are packed with information. First you see the current value within the last hour, then you see an upward or downward trend, and finally you see a sparkline (or trend line) that spans 24 hours.

The first row will now look similar to the following screenshot:

Real-time column charts with line overlays

It is time to build the second row of your real-time dashboard. Once again, we will use the cloning panel function:

1. Enter edit mode with **Edit | Edit Panels**.
2. Click **Add Panel**.
3. Clone the dynamic form-based dashboard: **Hits vs Response Time**:

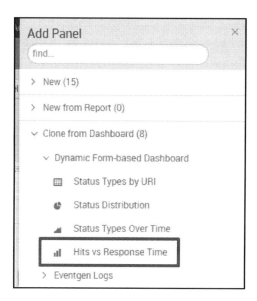

4. Click Add to Dashboard.

Do not be surprised if the graph is not generated. Remember we are cloning from a form-based dashboard with input tokens.

5. Rename the panel to `Traffic and Performance`.
6. Change the Search String to remove input token references:

```
SPL> index=main status_type="*" http_uri=* server_ip=*
        | timechart count, avg(http_response_time) as response_time
```

7. Change the **Time Range Scope** to **Explicit Selection**.
8. Change the **Time Range** to **Real-time** and set its value as **24 Hours Ago**.
9. Click on **Save**.
10. The chart will now populate the data.
11. Click on **Done**.

We will create another panel similar to the one we made previously. But this time, we will clone from the previous one to make our task easier.

1. Reload the browser. This is needed to load the newly-created panels in the clone selections.
2. Enter edit mode by **Edit | Edit Panels**.
3. Clone the **Hits vs Response Time** panel:

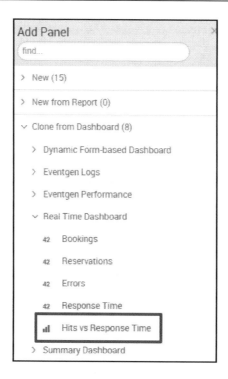

4. Rename the new panel to **Booking Conversion**.

5. Change the **Search String**:

```
SPL> index=main http_uri=/booking/reservation OR
     http_uri=/booking/confirmation
     | timechart count by http_uri | rename /booking/confirmation AS
     Confirmation, /booking/reservation AS Reservation
     | eval Conversion=Reservation/Confirmation
     | fields _time, Reservation, Confirmation, Conversion
```

6. Change **Time Range** to **Real-time | 24 Hours Ago**.

7. Click the **Visualization Options** dropdown.

8. Select the second option in **Stack Mode** as stacked.

9. Click **Chart Overlay**.

10. Delete the response_time overlay.

11. Add the **Conversion** overlay.

12. Turn on **View** as **Axis**.

13. Click on **Apply**.

14. Drag this panel to the right of the second row.

You have completed the real-time version of the combo charts. It should look similar to the following screenshot:

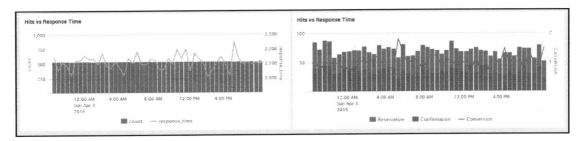

Real-time combo charts with line overlays

Creating a map called a choropleth

A choropleth, whose name comes from two Greek words meaning area/region and multitude, is a two-dimensional map where areas are designated by color shades or patterns to indicate the measured strength of a statistical indicator, such as sales per area or crime rates.

I'm sure you have already seen a choropleth, even if you didn't know what it was. Maybe you have seen areas of the US map shaded by state during a nationwide election. Or maybe you have seen a map of countries with a range of colors.

We cannot dig into the mathematical details of how a choropleth is created, but are fortunate that we can use Splunk 6.3+ to provide this effective visualization tool for us. We will create two choropleths to denote bookings by region and traffic by region.

Since we don't have a panel to clone from, we will create this from scratch:

1. Enter edit mode with **Edit | Edit Panels**.
2. Click on **Add Panel**.
3. Select **New | Choropleth Map**.
4. **Change Time Range** to **Real-time** and its value as **1 hour window**.
5. In **Content Title**, type in `Traffic Choropleth`.

6. Type in this **Search String**, which includes a geomap command and makes use of one of the two geographic lookup maps that are included by default with Splunk. The one used here includes the United States; the other one is for the world. This geomap command asks for a map with the counts for different states. Shading is based on the relative magnitudes of the counts:

```
SPL> index=main | iplocation client_ip | stats count by Region
       | rename Region as featureId | geom geo_us_states
```

7. Click on **Add to Dashboard**.
8. Click the **Visualization Options** dropdown.
9. We will now put the United States in the center of the map and adjust the zoom level.
10. Change **Latitude** to 39.
11. Change **Longitude** to -98.
12. Change **Zoom** to 4.

13. Click on the **Colors** tab.

14. **Change Number of Bins** to 9. This will increase the color range by adding more gradient tones:

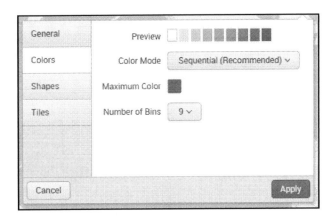

15. Click on **Apply**.
16. Click on **Done**.

Now reload your browser to allow this new panel to be added to the cloning panel selection.

Once you have cloned the **Traffic Choropleth** panel, change two things:

- **Title**: Bookings Choropleth
- **Search String**: index=main http_uri=/booking/confirmation http_status_code=200 | iplocation client_ip | stats count by Region | rename Region as featureId | geom geo_us_states

Now drag and position the second choropleth panel to the right of the other one to make the dashboard fluid.

You have now created a real-time single pane of glass dashboard. When you use this with your real production data, you can create a visualization that is useful and can produce all kinds of efficiencies. Your hard work can become a big hit!

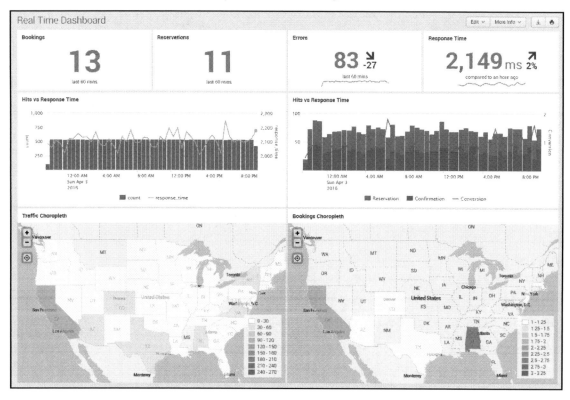

Dashboard with advanced indicators, combo charts with line overlays, and choropleth charts

Summary

In this chapter, you have delved deeper into dashboard creation. You have learned about the different types of dashboard and when to use them. You have created a fully functional form-based dashboard that allowed you to change the inputs and affect the dashboard data. You have also learned how to use tokens and assign them to search panels, and how to create and modify advanced visualization tools. Finally, you have learned how to create a real-time dashboard with advanced visualization panels such as Single Value Panels with Trends and Choropleths map. In the next chapter, Chapter 7, *Splunk SDK for JavaScript and D3.js*, you will learn to use the Splunk System Development Kit to make your visualizations even more interesting.

7

Splunk SDK for JavaScript and D3.js

In this chapter, we go on to learn about the Splunk **Software Development Kit (SDK)** and D3.js. Unlike previous chapters, here we will learn some special ways to interact with Splunk, ways that will allow us to create interesting and vibrant applications.

Specifically, in this chapter we will do the following:

- Learn about the Splunk SDK
- Discuss how the SDK can extract data from Splunk
- Find out how a website can be set up to show and use data extracted via the Splunk SDK
- Learn about another important software tool, D3.js, and how it can be used to create useful and impressive data visualizations

We'll begin by talking about Splunk SDKs and how they can be used.

Introduction to Splunk SDKs

A software development kit (also called a SDK or DevKit) is usually a set of software development tools that allows the creation of applications for a certain software package or software framework, but can also refer to a development kit for a computer system, operating system (OS), hardware platform, or even a video game system. We will use the Splunk SDK as a means of extracting data from Splunk and using it for external purposes (for example, a public website).

Splunk actually has several software development kits that sit on top of the REST API. These kits are for Python, Java, JavaScript, PHP, Ruby, and C#, and they allow developers to do all kinds of different things, such as integrating Splunk with third-party tools, logging directly into Splunk, extracting data to create archives, and others. They allow developers to do this using popular programming languages.

These Splunk SDKs do several specific tasks:

1. They handle HTTP access.
2. By utilizing a user ID and password, they authenticate the user.
3. They manage name spaces, which are the user and app context for accessing a resource, specified by a Splunk user name, a Splunk app, and a sharing mode.
4. They simplify access to REST endpoints, by making it easy to map a REST endpoint to a URI and HTTP method. (For more explanation, see `https://githu b.com/Mach-II/Mach-II-Framework/wiki/Introduction-to-REST-Endpoint s`.)
5. They build the appropriate URL for an endpoint.
6. Rather than providing the raw XML, JSON, or CSV, they return the events in a structure that has clear key-value pairs, thus simplifying the output for searches.

Practical applications of Splunk's SDK

In this chapter, we will show you how you can extract data from Splunk and display it externally through a web server without the need to log in to Splunk. This is extremely useful when the use case demands a real-time dashboard that is publicly displayed within your organization and that does not require logging in to Splunk.

To achieve this, we will use the Splunk SDK to extract the data from Splunk using a Node.js cron job and dump the payload into JSON files. A cron job involves the cron expressions we learned about in `Chapter 5`, *Data Optimization, Reports, Alerts, and Accelerating Searches*, which allow the developer to schedule alerts and other processes very precisely. The term *payload* is frequently used in computer programming to represent what the person receiving the output from the program is most interested in. The JSON files, which are files based on key-value pairs, will be served by a static web server. We will then create an HTML page with D3.js code that can utilize the JSON files to dynamically display the data in charts.

D3.js is an important tool for Splunk. It is a library, written in JavaScript, that uses data to change documents. It uses tools familiar to web designers, such as **Hypertext Markup Language (HTML)**, **Scalable Vector Graphics (SVG)**, and **Cascading Style Sheets (CSS)**, to create complex and effective visualizations. These visualizations are based on the **Document Object Model (DOM)**. The DOM is the interface used for HTML and XML documents and is used with a web browser. Using the DOM permits the developer to treat documents in a structured way, so that features can be duplicated throughout a website. In this way, a document's style, structure, and content can be easily manipulated.

We will not delve into the details of the Node.js programming language here. Suffice to say that it is an open source, cross-platform runtime environment designed for the development of server-side web applications. For more information, you can visit the website listed in the following *Prerequisites* section.

Prerequisites

There are several steps you need to take to prepare for using the Splunk SDK:

1. To add Node.js, download the Node.js framework (LTS version) from `https://n odejs.org/en/`. Check that you have successfully installed the Node.js framework by running this command in the Windows command prompt. The command returns the version; your version may be different:

   ```
   C:\> node -v
       V5.1.1
   ```

2. Create your working directory:

   ```
   C:\> mkdir dashboard
   C:\> cd dashboard
   ```

3. Install the Splunk SDK using the **Node Package Manager (npm)**:

   ```
   C:\> C:\dashboard> npm install splunk-sdk
   ```

   This will create a `node_modules` directory that will contain the Splunk SDK for the JavaScript package and all its dependencies. Ignore any warnings.

4. Install the `cron` package, which will allow us to run scheduled jobs. Again, you will use the **Node Package Manager (npm)**. Ignore any warnings:

   ```
   C:\> C:\dashboard> npm install cron
   ```

5. Choose a text editor that works for you. We recommend the Atom text editor from `https://atom.io/`. Go there now, download the Windows installer, and launch Atom.

6. You may download the code used in this chapter from the following link or use Git to clone it:

   - `https://github.com/ericksond/splunk-external-dashboard`
   - Git clone `https://github.com/ericksond/splunk-external-dashboard.git`

Creating a CRON Job

The CRON package allows us to use six or seven subexpressions to set up a scheduled alert. First, let us create something basic that will show us how to use the `cron` package to invoke a function. Using Atom or another text editor of choice, create a new file in the `c:\dashboard` directory and call it `jobs.js`. Paste the following code into the new file and save it:

```
// c:\dashboard\jobs.js

// require packages
var CronJob = require('cron').CronJob

// create a basic function
function hello_splunk() {
  console.log('hello splunk. give me your data.')
}

// create a cron job that executes the hello_splunk
// function every 5 seconds
new CronJob('*/5 * * * * *', function() {
  hello_splunk()
}, function() {
  // execute when job stops
}, true)
```

Now run this script using the Node interpreter:

```
C:\> C:\dashboard> node jobs.js
```

The code will not terminate and will continuously emit the message every 5 seconds. You learned how to create `cron` schedules in Splunk in `Chapter 5`, *Data Optimization, Reports, Alerts, and Accelerating Searches*. The same principle we used there applies here.

We will use this to query a Splunk saved search every few minutes and generate a JSON file out of the resulting data. In production scenarios, this is how often you want to query Splunk using the SDK. Later on, you will see that the code to query Splunk will include the username and password. This makes sense; if you use the SDK in a client-side JavaScript file, then anyone who knows how to open a JavaScript file could see the authentication credentials.

But for now, we need to stop the message or it will just keep going. To halt the execution of the Node script, hit *Ctrl + C* in the command window.

Creating a saved search

Next, we will create a saved search that we will eventually use to create a visualization. Follow these steps carefully:

1. Open Splunk and select the Destinations app.
2. Click **Settings | Searches, reports, and alerts**. Click on **New**.
3. Ensure that the **Destinations** app is selected.
4. In **Search Name**, type `sdk_status_codes`.
5. In the **Search**, type this:

   ```
   SPL> index=main | timechart span=1h count by http_status_code
   ```

6. In **Start time**, type `-24h@h`.
7. In **Finish time**, type `now`.
8. Click the checkbox for **Accelerate this search**. Select **7 Days**.

9. Use the following screenshot as a guide, then click **Save**:

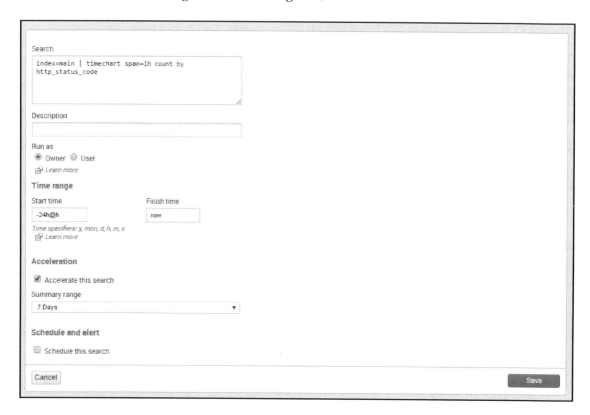

Creating the final dashboard\jobs.js

Here is the final `jobs.js` file we will use. Copy this block of code and overwrite the current `jobs.js` file. We will break this down into functions later and try to explain what the coding does, without putting too much emphasis on the Node.js code itself.

WARNING

When copying from PDF and other files, the encoding may be different, such that it breaks the apostrophes and quotation marks. If you encounter this, just search and replace all apostrophes (`'`) and quotation marks (`"`).

```
var CronJob = require('cron').CronJob
var splunkjs = require('splunk-sdk')
```

```
var fs = require('fs')

new CronJob('*/30 * * * * *', function() {
  // fetch the saved searchName
  fetchSavedSearch(renderResults, 'sdk_status_codes')
}, function() {}, true)

var service = new splunkjs.Service({
  username:"admin",
  password:"changed", // Use your own admin password
  scheme:"https",
  host:"localhost",
  port:"8089",
  version:"6.4"
});

function renderResults(data, searchName) {
  console.log(data)  // print out the result in the console
  fs.writeFile(__dirname + '/public/'+searchName+'.json',
JSON.stringify(data),
  function (err) {
    if (err) throw err
    console.log(new Date() + ' Written ' + searchName + '.json')
  })
}

function fetchSavedSearch(callback, searchName) {
  var savedSearches = service.savedSearches({
      owner: "admin",
      app: "destinations"
  });
  savedSearches.fetch(function (err, savedSearches) {
    if (err) {
      console.log(err)
      callback('error', searchName)
    } else {
      if (savedSearches.item(searchName) != null) {
        var savedSearch = savedSearches.item(searchName)
        savedSearch.dispatch({
            force_dispatch: false,
          }, function(e, job) {
          if (e) {
            console.log(e)
            callback('error', searchName)
          } else {
            job.setTTL(60, function(err, job) {});
            job.track({
              period: 200
```

```
        }, {
          done: function(job) {
            job.results({
              count: 0
            }, function(err, results, job) {
              console.log('Job Succeeded: ' + searchName)
              callback({
                fields: results.fields,
                rows: results.rows
              }, searchName)
            });
          },
          failed: function(job) {
            console.log("Job failed")
            callback('failed', searchName)
          },
          error: function(err) {
            console.log(err);
            callback('error', searchName)
          }
        })
      }
    })
  }
  }
})
}
```

Be sure you have altered the password changed to reflect your actual
admin password.

Before you actually run the previous code, you will need to first create a public directory: –
c:\dashboard\public. In production work, code should be resilient enough to generate a
directory if it needs it. However, we will not go over how to do that in this book; instead we
will make a new public directory the traditional way, by using the mkdir command in the
command window:

C:\> C:\dashboard> mkdir public

Now let us break the code down into sections to examine what it is doing:

```
// require packages
var CronJob = require('cron').CronJob
var splunkjs = require('splunk-sdk')
var fs = require('fs')
```

In this first code block, you are loading a Node.js module. You declare the variables CronJob, splunkjs, and fs, and then use require to read the JavaScript file, execute it, and return the export objects. These modules are the fundamental building blocks of Node.js and they are mapped directly to files. Remember they are located in the node_modules directory.

The important thing to take from this is that you are instantiating an object of the particular module. If the modules export objects, then you can access the exported functions via dot notation. Here is an example:

```
splunkjs.Service()
```

Let's go on to the next section:

```
// cron job runs every 30 sec
new CronJob('*/30*****',function() {
  // fetch the saved searchName
  fetchSavedSearch(renderResults, 'sdk_status_codes)
}, function() {}, true)
```

You have seen this before. This is the cron job. In this case, the cron job is scheduled to run every 30 seconds, executing the fetchSavedSearch() function in each iteration.

Note that the fetchSavedSearch() function takes two arguments. The first one is a callback function and the second is the saved search name.

Here is the next block of code:

```
// define the splunk service
var service=new splunkjs.Service({
  username:"admin",
  password:"changed", // Use your own admin account
  scheme: "https",
  host: "localhost",
  port:"8089",
  version:"6.4",
  });
```

This code block is now using the Splunk SDK to declare a service. The data you see is straightforward and includes the basic information required to connect to Splunk.

This is the main reason why you should not create the SDK on a JavaScript file as part of your website. You do not want this information exposed to your users or the cloud. By creating a cron jobs file, you can safely run it on the server without exposing this information.

In this block, we will render the results of the saved search and write the results to a JSON file:

```
// render the results of the saved search as part of the callback
// and write the payload to a JSON file
function renderResults(data, searchName) {
  console.log(data) //print out the result in the console
  // generate the json file
  fs.writeFile(_dirname + '/public/'+searchName+'.json',
JSON.stringify(data),
  function(err) {
    if (err) throw err
    console.log(new Date() + 'Written ' + searchName + '.json'
  })
}
```

The `renderResults()` function is responsible for printing the result of the saved search to the console and writing it into a JSON file. To achieve this, we used the native Node.js **File System** module (**fs**). The code expects that a public directory has been created beforehand. The code for the `fetchSavedSearch` function is listed below:

```
// fetch saved searches function
function fetchSavedSearch(callback, searchName) {
  var savedSearches=service.savedSearches({
      owner: "admin",
      app: "destinations"
  });
  savedSearches.fetch(function (err, savedSearches) {
    if (err) {
      console.log(err)
      callback('error', searchName)
    } else {
      if (savedSearches.item(searchName) != null) {
        var savedSearch = savedSearches.item(searchName)
        savedSearch.dispatch({
            force_dispatch: false,
          }, function(e, job) {
          if (e) {
            console.log(e)
            callback('error', searchName)
          } else {
```

```
        job.setTTL(60, function(err, job) {});
        job.track({
          period: 200
        }, {
          done: function(job) {
            job.results({
              count: 0
            }, function(err, results, job) {
              console.log('Job Succeeded: ' + searchName)
              callback({
                fields: results.fields,
                rows: results.rows
              }, searchName)
            });
          },
          failed: function(job) {
            console log("Job failed")
            callback('failed', searchName)
          },
          error: function(job) {
            console.log(err);
            callback('error', searchName)
          }
        })
      }
    })
  }
}
```

This function (fetchSavedSearch) does the bulk of the work for you. First, the function takes two arguments, a callback function and the saved search name. Read about JavaScript callbacks on the web to better understand them. (One place to look is https://www.sitepoint.com/demystifying-javascript-closures-callbacks-iifes/.) It might take a while to get your head around it, especially if you are more experienced in programming languages that do not treat functions as first-class objects. In JavaScript, you can pass around functions as objects. This is an important concept because JavaScript is asynchronous and will run functions independently of each other concurrently, unlike other programming languages that interpret the code consecutively.

The function takes in two arguments: the callback function and saved search name string:

```
fetchSavedSearch(renderResults, 'sdk_status_codes')
```

What this means is that anytime you see a `callback()` function executed within the `fetchSavedSearch()` function, it will actually invoke the `renderResults()` function and pass all arguments to it.

You can optionally add more saved searches by simply creating a second line of this function invocation, for example:

```
fetchSavedSearch(renderResults, 'my_second_saved_search')
```

Since the saved search name is being passed around, it will even make sure that the JSON file name is the same as the saved search name.

Now go ahead and run the job, and wait for about 30 seconds for the first run:

```
C:\> C:\dashboard> node jobs.js
```

Every time the cron executes, it will print the result of the saved search to the console. It will also tell you that it has successfully written the JSON file inside the `public` directory:

```
{ fields: [ '_time', 'count', '_span' ],
  rows:
   [ [ '2016-05-19T09:00:00.000-04:00', '0', '3600' ],
     [ '2016-05-19T10:00:00.000-04:00', '0', '3600' ],
     [ '2016-05-19T11:00:00.000-04:00', '0', '3600' ],
     [ '2016-05-19T12:00:00.000-04:00', '0', '3600' ],
     [ '2016-05-19T13:00:00.000-04:00', '0', '3600' ],
     [ '2016-05-19T14:00:00.000-04:00', '0', '3600' ],
     [ '2016-05-19T15:00:00.000-04:00', '0', '3600' ],
     [ '2016-05-19T16:00:00.000-04:00', '0', '3600' ],
     [ '2016-05-19T17:00:00.000-04:00', '0', '3600' ],
     [ '2016-05-19T18:00:00.000-04:00', '0', '3600' ],
     [ '2016-05-19T19:00:00.000-04:00', '0', '3600' ],
     [ '2016-05-19T20:00:00.000-04:00', '0', '3600' ],
     [ '2016-05-19T21:00:00.000-04:00', '0', '3600' ],
     [ '2016-05-19T22:00:00.000-04:00', '0', '3600' ],
     [ '2016-05-19T23:00:00.000-04:00', '0', '3600' ],
     [ '2016-05-20T00:00:00.000-04:00', '0', '3600' ],
     [ '2016-05-20T01:00:00.000-04:00', '0', '3600' ],
     [ '2016-05-20T02:00:00.000-04:00', '0', '3600' ],
     [ '2016-05-20T03:00:00.000-04:00', '0', '3600' ],
     [ '2016-05-20T04:00:00.000-04:00', '0', '3600' ],
     [ '2016-05-20T05:00:00.000-04:00', '0', '3600' ],
     [ '2016-05-20T06:00:00.000-04:00', '1', '3600' ],
     [ '2016-05-20T07:00:00.000-04:00', '12', '3600' ],
     [ '2016-05-20T08:00:00.000-04:00', '10', '3600' ],
     [ '2016-05-20T09:00:00.000-04:00', '13', '3600' ] ] }
Fri May 20 2016 09:47:31 GMT-0400 (Eastern Daylight Time) :: Successfully written JSON file: sdk_good_bookings.json
```

You can terminate the job with *Ctrl* + *C*. Later in the chapter, we will instruct you to turn it on again so we can see the real data stream against the D3 charts.

HTTP server

Now that we have the JSON file available in the `public` directory, it is time to make it live using a web server.

Install the `http-server` module with this command:

```
C:\> C:\dashboard> npm install http-server -g
```

The `-g` flag will ensure that this module is available globally, regardless of your current directory.

Now serve the files in the `public` directory with this command:

```
C:\> C:\dashboard> http-server -p 8080 C:\dashboard\public
```

Windows Firewall may prompt you to allow this app to use the port. Click on **Allow** access.

Now open a browser and go to the following URL: `http://localhost:8080`. If for some reason you have an application that uses port `8080`, change it to something else (for example, `9999`).

You will know that it works when you see the page shown in the following screenshot:

Note that you can just as easily click on the `sdk_status_codes.json` link and download it to your machine, just like any Internet object.

You now have your very own static web server. We will use this for the entire duration of the chapter to host the HTML and JavaScript files.

```
dashboard\public\index.html
```

For this to work, make sure you are using a modern browser (Google Chrome, Safari, or Firefox) and ensure that you have updated it.

Create a new document in `c:\dashboard\public` and name it `index.html`. Type in or copy this into the file:

```html
<!-- c:\dashboard\public\index.html -->
<!doctype html>
<head>
  <title>Real Time Dashboard</title>
  <link rel="stylesheet" href="/status_codes_chart.css"></style>
</head>
<body>
  <h3>Real Time Dashboard</h3>
  <div id="status_codes_chart"></div>
  <script src="https://d3js.org/d3.v3.min.js" charset="utf-8"></script>
  <script src="/status_codes_chart.js"></script>
</body>
</html>
```

We are including the online version of the D3.v3 script in the script declaration. We also need to create a new `status_codes_chart.js` file. Go ahead and do it now. Writing D3.js is beyond the scope of this book, but we will highlight the most important parts of this code block in the event that you wish to customize it. If you are reading this in a book, download the source code from GitHub.

You can find the code in the URL or simply clone the Git repository at `https://github.com/ericksond/splunk-external-dashboard`.

```javascript
// c:\dashboard\public\status_codes_chart.js
(function() {
  var chartId = '#status_codes_chart'
  var margin = {top: 60, right: 50, bottom: 20, left: 20}
  var width = parseInt(d3.select(chartId).style('width')) - margin.left -
    margin.right
  var height = parseInt(d3.select(chartId).style('height')) - margin.top -
    margin.bottom
  //var width = 600;
  //var height = 300;

  var x = d3.scale.ordinal()
      .rangeRoundBands([0, width]);

  var y = d3.scale.linear()
      .rangeRound([height, 0]);

  var z = d3.scale.category10();
```

```
    var xAxis = d3.svg.axis()
        .scale(x)
        .orient("bottom")
        .tickFormat(d3.time.format("%I:%M"))

    var yAxis = d3.svg.axis()
        .scale(y)
        .orient("right")

    var svg = d3.select(chartId).append("svg")
        .attr("width", width + margin.left + margin.right)
        .attr("height", height + margin.top + margin.bottom)
        .append("g")
        .attr("transform", "translate(" + margin.left + "," +
            margin.top + ")");

    var categories = ["200", "301", "302", "404", "500"]

    drawChart()

    function drawChart() {
        d3.json('/sdk_status_codes.json', function(error, json) {
        if (error) return console.warn(error)
        var data = []
        for(var i = 0; i < json.rows.length; i++) {
            data.push({
                "date": new Date(json.rows[i][0]),
                "200": parseInt(json.rows[i][1]),
                "301": parseInt(json.rows[i][2]),
                "302": parseInt(json.rows[i][3]),
                "404": parseInt(json.rows[i][4]),
                "500": parseInt(json.rows[i][5])
            })
        }

        var layers = d3.layout.stack()(categories.map(function(c) {
            return data.map(function(d) {
                return {x: d.date, y: d[c]}
            })
        }))

        x.domain(layers[0].map(function(d) { return d.x; }));
        y.domain([0, d3.max(layers[layers.length - 1], function(d) {
                return d.y0 + d.y; })]).nice();

        xAxis.tickValues(x.domain().filter(function(d, i) { return !(i % 3);
}))
```

```
    var layer = svg.selectAll(".layer")
        .data(layers)
      .enter().append("g")
        .attr("class", "layer")
        .style("fill", function(d, i) { return z(i); })

    layer.selectAll("rect")
        .data(function(d) { return d; })
      .enter().append("rect")
        .transition()
        .delay(function(d, i) {
          return i * 20
        })
        .duration(200)
        .attr("x", function(d) { return x(d.x); })
        .attr("y", function(d) { return y(d.y + d.y0); })
        .attr("height", function(d) { return y(d.y0) - y(d.y + d.y0); })
        .attr("width", x.rangeBand() - 1)

    layer.selectAll("text")
        .data(function(d) { return d; })
      .enter().append("text")
        .text(function(d) { if (d.y > 50) { return d.y }; } )
        .attr({
          'text-anchor': 'middle',
          x: function(d, i) { return x(d.x) + x.rangeBand() / 2 },
          y: function(d) { return y(d.y + d.y0) + 12 },
          'font-family': 'sans-serif',
          'font-size': '9px',
          fill: '#fff'
        })

    var legend = svg.selectAll(".legend")
        .data(categories)
      .enter().append("g")
        .attr("class", "legend")
        .attr("transform", function(d, i) {
            return "translate(" + i * -120 + ", 15)"; } )

    legend.append("rect")
        .attr({
          "x": width - 18,
          "y": -50,
          "width": 18,
          "height": 18,
        })
        .style("fill", function(d, i) { return z(i); } )
```

```
    legend.append("text")
        .attr({
          "x": width - 24,
          "y": -41,
          "dy": ".35em",
          "font-size": "11px",
          "font-face": "sans-serif",
          "fill": "#999"
        })
        .style("text-anchor", "end")
        .text(function(d) { return d; })

  svg.append("g")
      .attr("class", "axis axis--x")
      .attr("transform", "translate(0," + height + ")")
      .attr("fill", "#999")
      .transition()
      .delay(function(d, i) {
        return i * 50
      })
      .duration(500)
      .call(xAxis);

  svg.append("g")
      .attr("class", "axis axis--y")
      .attr("transform", "translate(" + width + ",0)")
      .attr("fill", "#999")
      .transition()
      .delay(function(d, i) {
        return i * 50
      })
      .duration(500)
      .call(yAxis);

    });
  }
})()
```

If you wish to learn how to write D3.js scripts, go to `https://d3js.org/`.

We will now highlight the different parts of the JavaScript file:

```
(function() {
  var chartId = '#status_codes_chart'
  var margin = {top: 60, right: 50, bottom: 20, left: 20}
  var width = parseInt(d3.select(chartId).style('width')) - margin.left -
    margin.right
  var height = parseInt(d3.select(chartId).style('height')) - margin.top -
```

```
      margin.bottom
   //var width = 600;
   //var height = 300;
  ...
 })()
```

This is the entry point of the script. Here you are declaring the `div` ID
`status_codes_chart` that matched the one in the `index.html` file. The margins are also
being defined here. The width and height can either be dynamically assigned (first set) or
statically assigned (second set). If dynamically assigned, they will either fall back to the
width and height defined in the CSS, or they will adjust based on the window size. Feel free
to tweak this later on and see how the chart changes:

```
var x = d3.scale.ordinal()
    .rangeRoundBands([0, width]);

var y = d3.scale.linear()
    .rangeRound([height, 0]);

var z = d3.scale.category10();

var xAxis = d3.svg.axis()
    .scale(x)
    .orient("bottom")
    .tickFormat(d3.time.format("%I:%M"))

var yAxis = d3.svg.axis()
    .scale(y)
    .orient("right")
```

This block of code consists of D3 elements that are being declared. Suffice to say that these
are required to create the SVG screenshot needed by the chart:

```
var svg = d3.select(chartId).append("svg")
    .attr("width", width + margin.left + margin.right)
    .attr("height", height + margin.top + margin.bottom)
    .append("g")
    .attr("transform", "translate(" + margin.left + "," +
        margin.top + ")");

var categories = ["200", "301", "302", "404", "500"]

drawChart()
```

The previous block of code is D3 creating the SVG object. Notice that `d3.select(chartId)` is actually equal to `d3.select("#status_codes_chart")`. This is telling the D3 script to create the SVG chart in that `div`.

The `var categories[]` array defines what fields will be shown in the chart. These numbers are the result of the query that you ran against Splunk. If you wish to omit a particular status code from the resulting bar chart, then remove it from this list. The list requires a minimum of one entry.

`drawChart()` is a function call, which we will show you now.

The `drawChart()` function will contain all the instructions to generate the data based on the JSON object that is being called through the `d3.json()` method:

```
function drawChart() {
    d3.json('/sdk_status_codes.json', function(error, json) {
      if (error) return console.warn(error)
      var data = []
      for(var i = 0; i < json.rows.length; i++) {
        data.push({
          "date": new Date(json.rows[i][0]),
          "200": parseInt(json.rows[i][1]),
          "301": parseInt(json.rows[i][2]),
          "302": parseInt(json.rows[i][3]),
          "404": parseInt(json.rows[i][4]),
          "500": parseInt(json.rows[i][5])
        })
      }
```

The `d3.json` call essentially makes a GET request against the URL of our local JSON file, which then passes the data back to the function.

The `for` loop here is not part of D3.js. This is just needed to format the incoming data to match the data needed by D3:

```
var layers = d3.layout.stack()(categories.map(function(c) {
    return data.map(function(d) {
      return {x: d.date, y: d[c]}
    })
  }))
```

This block of code creates the layers of the chart.

```
dashboard\public\status_codes_chart.css
```

The source for this is at https://github.com/ericksond/splunk-external-dashboard.

Create a new CSS file in c:\dashboard\public and name it status_codes_chart.css:

```css
text {
  font-family: monospace;
}

.axis text {
  font: 10px sans-serif;
}

.axis line,
.axis path {
  fill: none;
  stroke: #ccc;
  shape-rendering: crispEdges;
}

.axis--x path {
  display: none;
}

#status_codes_chart {
  -webkit-touch-callout: none;
  -webkit-user-select: none;
  -khtml-user-select: none;
  -moz-user-select: none;
  -ms-user-select: none;
  user-select: none;
  /* Trying to get SVG to act like a greedy block in all browsers */
  display: block;
  width:50%;
  height:400px;
}
```

Rendering the chart

Now that all the components are in place, reload the page and check the result at `http://localhost:8080`.

If this page is not loading, make sure the `http-server` process is running. Refer to the earlier sections in this chapter for how to run the `http-server`:

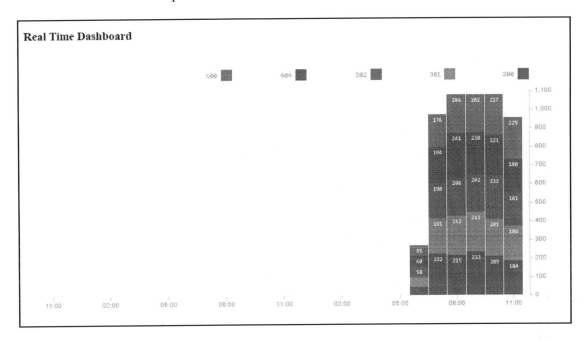

Now you have a stacked bar chart that is being fed with data from Splunk. Go ahead and run the `jobs.js` cron job again using the following command. You need to do this in a separate command prompt window:

```
C:\> C:\dashboard> node jobs.js
```

Wait a few minutes and refresh the page. See it change before your eyes. There are many ways to make this dynamically update in real time. You can use JavaScript or browser-based refresh plugins. You may also extend the D3.js code and create a `redrawChart()` function that updates certain data entry points. The important thing is that you can now create public dashboards that will display data from Splunk without the need to log in to the application. You will be in total control of this dashboard as well.

Summary

In this chapter, we showed you how to use the Splunk SDK to safely extract data from Splunk using JavaScript without the risk of exposing authentication credentials to viewers. You have also learned how to use Node.js and the npm. Additionally, you wrote a cron script that pulls data from Splunk and writes it into a local JSON file. And you used the `http-server` module to initialize a lightweight web server. Finally, you created the web application using D3.js to display a stacked bar chart using Splunk data. In the next chapter, Chapter 8, *HTTP Event Collector*, you will go on to learn about this event collector and how it can be used for many business purposes.

8
HTTP Event Collector

In this chapter, we will learn about the **HTTP Event Collector** (HEC) that was released with Splunk v6. This addition has added a new way for websites and their processes to be monitored and improved.

In this chapter we will learn about the following topics:

- What is the HEC?
- How does the HEC work to improve website operations by sending HTTP and HTTPS events directly from an application to Splunk?
- How data flows to the HEC
- How to generate an HEC token
- How to perform a POST request by placing the EC token in the request's authentication header
- How to POST data (in JSON format) to the receiver for the HEC token
- How to send data to the HEC using Web UI click events
- How to log on to the HEC with JavaScript

What is the HEC?

Splunk (in versions 6.0 and up) has created a very useful data tool that is important for Splunk developers to be aware of. The HEC has the important function of collecting and sending HTTP and HTTPS events directly from a web application to Splunk, where it can then be used for analysis, creating alerts, and other effective functions of Splunk.

How does the HEC work?

HTTP and HTTPS events created by web applications contain event metadata, such as time, host, source, source type, and index, as well as other event data, found in curly brackets following the *event* key. The HEC makes it easy for app developers to add a minimal amount of code in order to send this data, so it's valuable for operational decision making, directly from their apps to Splunk. This is all done in a secure and efficient way, making it easy for apps to be able to Splunk their data.

Typically, an application generates its own log file or uses **Document Object Model (DOM)** tagging to generate some relevant functional metrics. This is useful and still applicable to traditional multi-page web applications. But web page development has leapt forward in recent years with a new framework called **Single Page Application (SPA)**. The advance of SPA means that most of an application's work in showing HTML results now happens dynamically in the client's browser. Instead of going through different HTML pages, only one HTML page is loaded when the user interacts with the app.

This advance, though revolutionary, can pose a crucial dilemma for data monitoring. Since most of the application's interactions now occur on the client side, no server-side tracking can be done. This is where the HEC comes into its own, since you can create a very small line of JavaScript code that can essentially push data into Splunk. It is important to be aware that for applications in the cloud, this will only work if you are using Splunk Cloud or if your Splunk instance is accessible in the public domain.

There are use cases other than web applications that may also find the HEC useful. For internal applications, the HEC can easily be utilized to keep track of events occurring in the client's UI. This is also viable for the increasingly ubiquitous **Internet of Things** (known as **IoT**, a network of devices with a variety of purposes that is hooked up to a network). This is also a good way to monitor mobile applications.

How data flows to the HEC?

Let's begin by looking at how data flows to the HEC. This is a multi-step process that is important to understand before we go deeper.

Logging in data

First, data needs to be logged in, but before that it needs to be packaged from the source, which can be done in a number of different ways. These are listed as follows:

- A Splunk logging library, such as Splunk logging for Java or Splunk logging for .NET
- Another agent, such as a JavaScript request library
- The Java Apache HTTP client
- And lastly, some other client, as long as it will appropriately package the event data in JSON format

Before going further, let's review what the JSON format means. A couple of examples of key-value pairs in JSON format are shown here. The key is listed first, then a colon, then the value of that key. Sequences of key-value pairs must be separated by commas:

```
"time": 1636289537,
"index": "main",
```

Using a token with data

Second, the system needs to take each JSON data package and give it the same token in its authorization header. This will enable data to be brought into Splunk. The fact that the system is based on tokens means that the user doesn't have to include Splunk credentials in the application or in files that support the application. This token has been generated by Splunk in preparation for bringing in the data. It is created using the management endpoint or the Splunk Enterprise management URI and one of the following tools:

- The HEC user interface
- cURL, which is a way to use a BASH script to get information from a URL
- The Splunk **command-line interface (CLI)**

Sending out the data request

Third, the JSON data packages, each of which has its correct token, are then sent out as an HTTP or HTTPS request to the input endpoint on the instance of Splunk Enterprise.

Verifying the token

Fourth, the token is checked and verified against the list of known tokens. If it passes this checkpoint, and is found to be a good token, then the data package is taken in by Splunk.

Indexing the data

Fifth, the data is taken by Splunk from the JSON packet payload and is indexed. It can then be analyzed and examined.

We hope that by going over the preceding steps, you can begin to see how the HEC process we have just discussed can help an organization find operational efficiencies and uncover ways to improve functioning. Let's now get started with exactly how to do this, step by step.

We will show you specifically how Splunk can be used to improve the functioning of a web company. You will learn to do the following:

- Enable the HEC
- Create an authentication token
- Perform a basic POST request with the HEC token using PowerShell
- Verify the request and response
- Use the JavaScript logging library to interface with HEC.

Enabling the HEC

In this section, we'll talk about the HEC and how to enable it, because, as we noted in the preceding section, it is not, by default, enabled. The HEC was created with the Splunk user in mind, as a way to make the transfer of large amounts of data from web applications to Splunk much easier. To enable the HEC in your local Splunk instance, perform the following steps, after which you can refer the following screenshot:

1. Click on **Settings | Data Inputs**.
2. Click on **HTTP Event Collector**.
3. Click on the **Global Settings** button in the upper-right corner of the page.
4. Enable **All Tokens**.
5. In the **Default Source Type**, type `access_custom`.
6. In the **Default Index**, type `main`.

7. Uncheck **Enable SSL** for our testing purposes only. This is not recommended in production.
8. Leave the rest at the default settings.

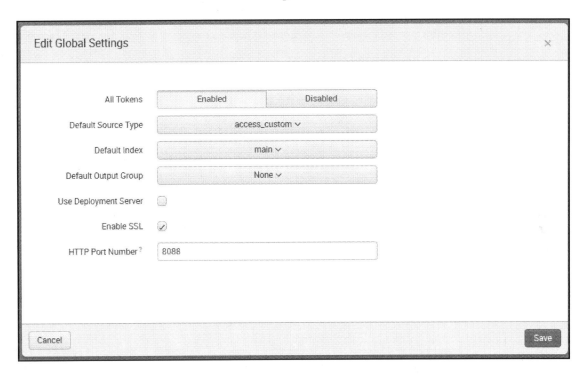

Generating an HEC authentication token

Next, you will need to generate an HEC authentication token. The HEC token will ensure that no unknown applications will be able to send data to Splunk. This HEC authentication token will be sent in the HTTP headers of the incoming request to Splunk. Without this token, the response would typically indicate a status code 401 (Unauthorized error).

The HEC token will also enable you to override the source tag of all incoming data. This makes it easy to differentiate data streams later, based on where the data is coming from. It is best practice to create a separate token for each application. If something goes wrong with one application, say it started flooding your Splunk instance with unwanted data, it will then be easy enough to disable that associated token to mitigate the issue. Follow these instructions:

1. Click **Settings | Data Inputs**.

2. Find **HTTP Event Collector**.

3. Click **New Token**.

4. In the **Name** field, enter `Demo1`.

5. Leave the other fields as-is.

6. Click **Next** to proceed.

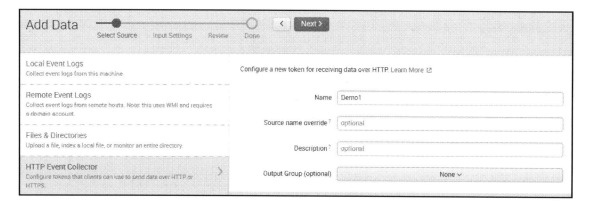

You will see an **Input Settings** page that looks like the following screenshot. Follow these instructions:

1. In the **Input Settings** page, you will create a new **Source Type**.

2. In the first **Source type** section, click **New**.

3. Type `ec_demo1` as the **Source Type**.

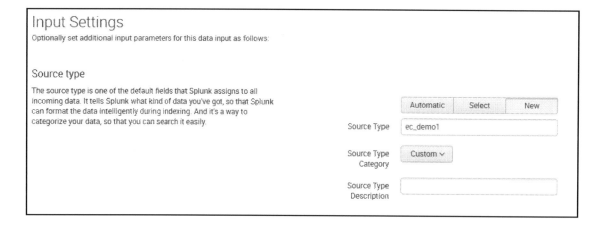

4. In the **Index** section, select **main** as the allowed index.
5. Select **main** as the **Default Index** as well.

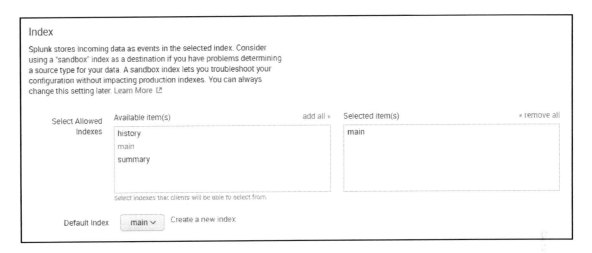

6. Click **Review** to proceed.
7. Verify your work against the following screenshot, then click on **Submit**.

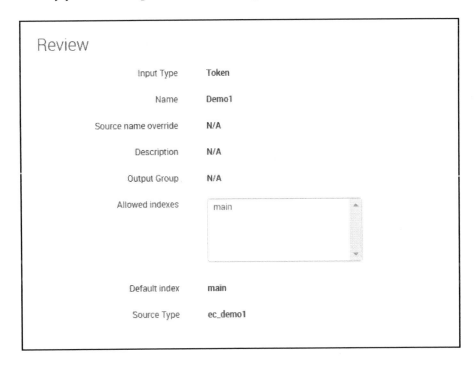

8. Once you are done, go back to **Data Inputs | HTTP Event Collector** and you should see the newly-generated **Token Value**. Copy or take note of this value as you will need it for the exercises in this chapter. This value is unique to every Splunk instance. An example of a token value is highlighted in the following image:

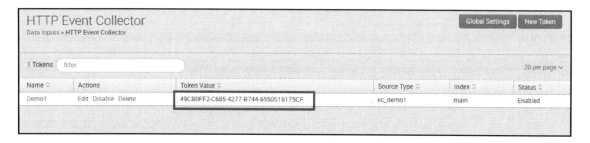

As you have learned in the previous chapters, everything that you change in the Splunk UI generally makes a change to a configuration file. In this case, the new EC Inputs modified the `c:\splunk\etc\apps\splunk_httpinput\local\inputs.conf` file with the upcoming content.

You need to modify this file now and add the **Cross Origin Resource Sharing (CORS)** policy. This will allow our REST API calls to the HEC to work later on. This is not necessarily done in a production environment.

Run this Windows command to create the `inputs.conf` file.

```
C:\> notepad c:\splunk\etc\apps\splunk_httpinput\local\inputs.conf
```

Modify the file by adding the highlighted line under the [http] stanza. Take note of the port in the URL; if you used a different port to launch your HTTP server, then make sure you change it here as well. We use port 8080 here because it is commonly used for this purpose, but check to make sure it is correct for your system:

```
[http]
disabled = 0
index = main
sourcetype = access_custom
enableSSL = 0
crossOriginSharingPolicy = http://localhost:8080

[http://Demo1]
disabled = 0
index = main
indexes = main
```

```
sourcetype = ec_demo1
token = 49CB0FF2-C685-4277-B744-6550516175CF
```

Restart Splunk for the changes to take effect:

```
C:\> c:\splunk\bin\splunk restart
```

How to test the HEC with cURL and PowerShell

Now we want to test the HEC. Here, we want to do a HEC POST request. Splunk will expect the information below, which is the basic information you need to make a successful HEC POST. Again, notice that the port used is 8088, which is commonly used, but this can be configured according to the needs of your system:

- **URL**: http://localhost:8088/services/collector
- **Custom Header**: Authorization
- **Custom Header Value**: Splunk <token>
- **Content Type**: application/json
- **Body**: { "event": "this is your message" }

An easy and quick way to test the HTTP event collector is using cURL (or curl, as it is sometimes written). cURL is included in Mac OS X and Linux, and helps to transfer data to or from a server. For this purpose, it can use one of many different protocols, including HTTP and HTTPS (we will give you another way this time using Windows in the following section).

Here is the command for cURL:

```
curl -k http://localhost:8088/services/collector -H 'Authorization: Splunk
<token>' -d '{"event":"this is your message"}'
```

Although doing a one-time test in cURL is convenient, it is not included in Windows by default and you cannot further enhance your test programmatically.

Since we wrote this book in the context of Windows users, let us use PowerShell, which is a Windows-based scripting language and automation platform that is helpful for managing your information systems. It uses the .NET platform to give you the functionality needed to help control your Windows systems.

To bring up PowerShell, use the following steps:

1. Do a search in your Windows machine for **Windows PowerShell ISE**.
2. Right-click it and select **Run as Administrator**.

Notice that the ISE will have two panels; the top one is where you write your script, and the bottom one, which is an actual PowerShell shell, is where you can execute commands. Once you create your script, a clickable **Run Script** icon will execute the script and return the output at the bottom panel. You can also press *F5* to execute the script.

Now, to move ahead with this exercise, perform the following steps:

1. Copy or write down the following script into the upper panel. Since all lines marked with a hash sign (#) are comments and are not executed, you can choose to include these or not.
2. Pay very close attention to the first statement, where you will need to replace **HEC TOKEN GOES HERE** with the token you have just generated. It is the one you were asked to save and write down previously.

```
# Change your HEC Token here
$token = 'HEC TOKEN GOES HERE'

# Disable SSL Validation
[System.Net.ServicePointManager]::ServerCertificateValidationCallback
= {$true}

# Create a dictionary object to contain the HTTP headers
$headers = New-Object
"System.Collections.Generic.Dictionary[[String],[String]]"

# Create an HTTP Authorization header with the EC Token
$headers.Add("Authorization", 'Splunk ' + $token)

# Create the JSON data that will be sent along with the POST request
$event = @{
  event="demo event 1"
}
$json = $event | ConvertTo-Json

# Initiate the POST request including the headers and the
```

```
    JSON payload
$response = Invoke-RestMethod
'http://localhost:8088/services/collector' -Method Post
-Body $json -ContentType 'application/json' -Headers $headers

# Echo the response
Write-Host $response
```

3. Again, remember, if you have any problems, before executing, you needed to swap the $token value as indicated with the one that was generated by the creation of the HEC Token, which you created with these steps earlier: **Settings | Data Inputs | HTTP Event Collector** (Token Value).

   Here, we have produced a screenshot of the final script with a token in the machine. You will also see this in the lab section in GitHub: `https://github.com /ericksond/splunk-essentials/tree/master/labs/chapter8`.

4. After you have replaced the token value, click the **Run Script** button highlighted in the following screenshot, or hit F5 on your keyboard.

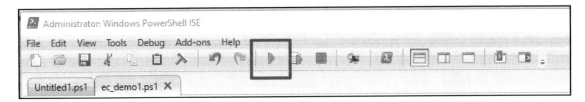

5. If all goes well, you should see the output of the script as follows:

   ```
   @{text=Success; code=0}
   ```

6. Now that you know how the testing works, go into Splunk and run the following search command:

   SPL> index=main sourcetype=ec_demo1

7. You should now see your events.

Although doing this test in PowerShell was a little more complex than a mere cURL command, any Windows admin can now use the very same script you wrote and for a more practical application. For example, you can use this base script to check the status of a particular application and based on the conditions, report it back to Splunk.

Using the HEC with dynamic UI events

In the previous chapter, we created a dashboard using D3.js that renders a chart with Splunk data in it. You also learned how to use the HTTP server module as a simple web server. We will use the same setup for the next exercise.

First, we will create a static HTML file with form buttons that we can click. Every click event will generate a Splunk HEC POST in the background to capture the details of the click event. *The code that follows is by no means secure and should not be used in production. This is for example purposes only.*

Create a new HTML file inside the c:\dashboard\public directory and call it ectest.html. Copy or type in the following contents of the HTML file:

```
<!-- c:\dashboard\public\ectest.html -->
<!doctype html>
<head>
  <title>EC Tester</title>
</head>
<body>
  <h3>HTTP Event Collector UI Tester</h3>
  <button type="button" id="btn1" onClick="splunkIt(this, 'Event 1 button
clicked.')">Click Event 1</button>
  <button type="button" id="btn1" onClick="splunkIt(this, 'Event 2 button
clicked.')">Click Event 2</button>
  <button type="button" id="btn1" onClick="splunkIt(this, 'Event 3 button
clicked.')">Click Event 3</button>
  <script src="/ectest.js"></script>
</body>
</html>
```

Now run the HTTP server. Open a command prompt, and type in the following command:

```
C:\> http-server -p 8080 c:\dashboard\public
```

Launch a browser tab and navigate to http://localhost:8080/ectest.html. The following screenshot shows how the page will look:

Now let us create the JavaScript file that will be monitoring the button click events and sending the HEC data to Splunk.

Create a new JavaScript file inside the `c:\dashboard\public` directory and call it `ectest.js`. Change the `ecToken` value in the first line of the JavaScript file to your own HEC token:

```
// public/ectest.js
var ecToken = '13EA3875-2879-4F44-AF0A-3ED336CB5BCA'

function splunkIt(object, clickEvent) {
  console.log(object, event);
  var xhr = new XMLHttpRequest();

  xhr.open('POST', 'http://localhost:8088/services/collector', true);
  xhr.setRequestHeader('Authorization', 'Splunk ' + ecToken);
  xhr.withCredentials = true;
  xhr.onload = function() {
    if (xhr.status === 200) {
      var userInfo = JSON.parse(xhr.responseText);
    }
  };
  xhr.send(JSON.stringify({
    event: clickEvent
  }));
};
```

Now that you have the JavaScript in place, reload your browser or navigate to the following URL again: `http://localhost:8080/ectest.html`. This was tested with Google Chrome.

You can open the Developer Tools and the JavaScript console within Google Chrome. The JavaScript console allows you to use basic JavaScript statements and commands specific to the console when the page is in the browser, thus allowing you to quickly and easily debug it. With the console, you can see any diagnostics, view both raw and structured data, filter and control the output, and modify various elements within the page.

Click the buttons and run the search query against Splunk. Set the time frame to a 5-minute window real time and watch the data flow in as soon as you click the buttons.

```
SPL> index=main sourcetype=ec_demo1
```

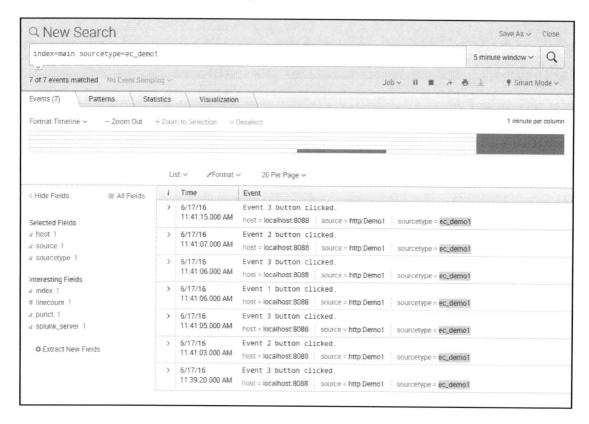

At this point, you have successfully created a web page that sends signals to Splunk every time a UI event is performed.

JavaScript logging with the HEC

Perhaps the best use case for using the HEC is with logging libraries. These allow the automatic collection of data when code is executing.

We will use the HEC Stream for Bunyan. Bunyan is a simple and fast JSON logging library for Node.js services. Here are additional references you can look at regarding these projects:

- Information about HTTP Event Collector Stream for Bunyan is present at `http://dev.splunk.com/view/splunk-logging-javascript/SP-CAAAE8A`
- Information about Bunyan is present at `https://github.com/trentm/node-bunyan`

The following sample code will inject an event to our initially defined HEC. Every time this is executed, it will create a Splunk event with a random number. You can find the complete code by cloning the external dashboard repository:

`https://github.com/ericksond/splunk-external-dashboard`

After cloning or unzipping the package, run this series of commands to install the dependencies:

```
C:\> git clone https://github.com/ericksond/splunk-external-dashboard.git
C:\> cd splunk-external-dashboard ( or cd dashboard)
C:\dashboard> npm install
C:\dashboard> notepad heclogging.js
```

Change the HEC token by replacing the value in this field:

```
var config = {
  token: "TOKEN GOES HERE",
  url: "http://localhost:8088"
};
```

Save the file then run the code:

```
C:\> node heclogging.js
```

If all goes well, you should see an output similar to this:

```
C:\> C:\dashboard>node heclogging.js
    Sending payload { event: 'logging event #0.8825588226318359' }
```

Now go back to Splunk and check if your data made it in:

```
SPL> index=main sourcetype=ec_demo1
```

Here is an example event that shows that the code worked:

```
List ∨        ⁄Format ∨      20 Per Page ∨

i   Time              Event

>   8/11/16           { [-]
    8:37:27.117 AM        message: { [-]
                              event: logging event #0.8825588226318359
                              msg: Posted successfully.
                              name: logger
                              pid: 5892
                              v: 0
                          }
                          severity: info
                      }
                      Show as raw text
                      host = WIN-DTI1F5NUKEN    source = http:Demo1    sourcetype = ec_demo1

>   8/11/16           { [-]
    8:19:31.565 AM        message: { [+]
                          }
                          severity: info
                      }
                      Show as raw text
                      host = WIN-DTI1F5NUKEN    source = http:Demo1    sourcetype = ec_demo1

>   8/11/16           { [-]
    8:18:48.394 AM        message: { [+]
                          }
                          severity: info
                      }
                      Show as raw text
                      host = WIN-DTI1F5NUKEN    source = http:Demo1    sourcetype = ec_demo1
```

Here is the complete working code for the `heclogging.js` file:

```javascript
var splunkBunyan = require("splunk-bunyan-logger");
var bunyan = require("bunyan");

var config = {
  token: "13EA3875-2879-4F44-AF0A-3ED336CB5BCA",
  url: "http://localhost:8088"
};
var splunkStream = splunkBunyan.createStream(config);

splunkStream.on("error", function(err, context) {
  console.log("Error", err, "Context", context)
```

```
});

var Logger = bunyan.createLogger({
    name: "logger",
    streams: [
        splunkStream
    ]
});

var payload = {
  event: "logging event #" + Math.random()
};

console.log("Sending payload", payload);
Logger.info(payload, "Posted successfully.")
```

You can retrieve the code files used in this chapter in the following GitHub repository: `https://github.com/ericksond/splunk-external-dashboard`.

Summary

In this chapter, you have learned about the HEC and how it can be used to send HTTP and HTTPS data directly from an application to Splunk. To do this, you learned how to create a token and generate a token key to be used to access the data. You have also learned how to use cURL (for MAC or Linux) and PowerShell (for Windows) to collect the data. And you have created a basic website with buttons that will send the events back to Splunk. Lastly, you have learned how to search the data you have collected from the application.

In the next chapter, we'll go on and learn about recommended ways to work with Splunk.

9

Best Practices and Advanced Queries

As we bring this book to a close, we want to leave you with a few extra skills in your Splunk toolkit. Throughout the book, you have gained the essential skills required to use Splunk effectively. In this chapter, we will look at some best practices that you can incorporate in your daily Splunk work. These include the following:

- Temporary indexes and oneshot indexing
- Searching within an index
- Searching within a limited time frame
- How to do quick searches via fast mode
- How to use event sampling
- Using the universal forwarder

We will also list some advanced SPL queries that you can use as templates when the need arises. These include:

- Doing a subsearch, or a search within a search
- Using `append` and `join`
- Using `eval` with `if`
- Using `eval` with `match`

Throughout this book, we have seen how logs can be used to improve applications and to troubleshoot problems. Since logs are such an important component of using data with Splunk, we end the chapter with a few basics, recommended by Splunk, that should be remembered when you are creating logs. These are:

- Include clear key-value pairs
- Create events that are understandable to human readers
- Remember to use timestamps for all events
- Be sure your identifiers are unique
- Log using text format, not binary
- Use formats that developers can easily use
- Log what you think might be useful at some point
- Create use categories with meaning
- Include the source of the log event
- Minimize the number of multi-line events

Temporary indexes and oneshot indexing

When you need to index new data and you are unfamiliar with its format, it is always best practice to use a temporary index. You should begin by creating a temporary index just for this purpose. Once you have this temporary index, you can use a Splunk command to add the file once. This process is called **oneshot** indexing. This is crucial when you know you have to transform the data prior to indexing, for instance when using props.conf and transforms.conf. A nice feature of oneshot indexing is that there is no need for any kind of configuration before uploading.

Here is how you perform oneshot indexing using the CLI:

```
C:\> c:\splunk\bin\splunk add oneshot TestFile.log —index TempIndex —
    sourcetype TempSourceType
```

You can also do this from the UI by going to **Settings** | **Data inputs** | **Files and Directories** | **Add new**. Then browse for the file and click on **Index Once**.

These methods will only work when Splunk is stopped. It will warn you if it is not. Once again, it is crucial that you indicate the specific index using the -index parameter. Without it, it will clean all indexes.

For example, to clean the index we created previously, we use the command you can see highlighted here:

```
C:\> c:\splunk\bin\splunk clean eventdata -index TempIndex
```

Searching within an index

Always remember to filter your searches by index. By doing so, you can dramatically speed up your searches. If you don't restrict your search to a specific index, it means Splunk has to go through all available indexes and execute the search against them, thus consuming unnecessary time.

When designing your Splunk implementation, partitioning of indexes is also very crucial. Careful thought needs to be taken when planning for the indexes and their partitioning. In my experience, it is best to create an index for every type of source included in your incoming data.

For example, all web server logs for the same application should be placed in one index. You may then split the log types by source type, but keep them within the same index. This will give you a generally favorable search speed even if you have to search between two different source types.

Here are some examples:

Index name	Source type
App1	Logs.Error
App1	Logs.Info
App1	Logs.Warning
App2	Logs.Error
App2	Logs.Info
App3	Logs.Warning

As you can see, we have indexed by app number first, then created various subtypes. You may then create a search query within the same index, even if you have to combine two source types:

- A good query will be as follows:

    ```
    SPL> index=App1 sourcetype=Logs.Error OR Logs.Warning
    ```

- A bad query will be as follows:

    ```
    SPL> sourcetype=Logs.* Error
    ```

The way we have set it up here, if you ever have to retrieve data from both indexes, then you can combine them with the following query. It is not as efficient as searching against a single index, but it is better than going through all other available indexes:

```
SPL> index=App1 OR index=App2 sourcetype=Logs.Error
```

Search within a limited time frame

By default, the Search and Reporting app's time range is set to `All Time`. Searches done using this time frame will have a negative performance impact on your Splunk instance. This is heightened when there are concurrent users doing the same thing. Although you can train your users to always select a limited time range, not everybody will remember to do this.

The solution for this problem is fairly simple. You can simply change the default time range for the drop-down menu. We will do this by modifying the `ui-prefs.conf` file in an administrative command prompt.

Go ahead and execute the following command:

```
C:\> notepad c:\Splunk\etc\system\local\ui-prefs.conf
```

Copy and paste the following into the file:

```
[search]
dispatch.earliest_time = -4h
dispatch.latest_time = now
[default]
dispatch.earliest_time = -4h
dispatch.latest_time = now
```

Save the file and restart Splunk. Go back to the **Search and Reporting** app and the default time range should now say **Last 4 hours**. Note that this will also change the default time range in the Search dashboard of the Destinations app, since any change in the default will be automatically applied to all apps, unless specified otherwise.

This is a good way to ensure that your users will not accidentally run search queries against all existing data without a time frame.

Quick searches via fast mode

There are three types of searching available for Splunk: **Fast Mode**, **Smart Mode**, and **Verbose Mode**:

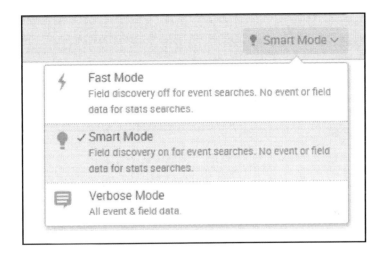

If you want your searches to be faster, use **Fast Mode**. Fast mode will not attempt to generate fields during search time, unlike the default smart mode. This is very good to use when you do not know what you are looking for. **Smart Mode** looks for **transforming commands** in your searches. If it finds these, it acts like fast mode; if it doesn't, then it acts like verbose mode. **Verbose Mode** means that the search will provide as much information as possible, even though this may result in significantly slower searches.

Using event sampling

New to version 6.4 is **event sampling**. Like the fact that you only need a drop of blood to test for the amount of sugar and sodium levels in your blood, you often only need a small amount of data from your dataset to make conclusions about that dataset. The addition of event sampling to the Splunk toolset is particularly useful, because there is often so much data available and what you are really seeking is to take measurements from that data quickly:

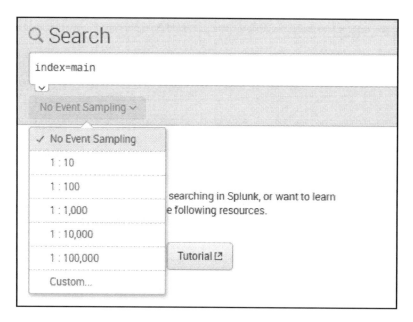

Event sampling uses a sample ratio value that reduces the number of results. If a typical search result returns 1,000 events, a 1:10 event sampling ratio will return 100 events. As you can see from the previous screenshot, these ratios can significantly cut the amount of data indexed, and can range from a fairly large ratio (which can be set using the **Custom** setting) to one as small as 1:100,000 (or even smaller, again using the **Custom** setting).

This is not suitable for saved searches for which you need accurate counts. This is, however, perfect when you are testing your search queries as they will return significantly faster. Most of the time you will spend in Splunk is taken up with trying and retrying queries using SPL. If you have to deal with a large amount of data all the time, then your work time will be slow. Remember to use event sampling, and you will reduce the time it takes to create useful searches.

The following steps indicate the steps you should take in this process:

- Do a quick search to ensure that the correct data is present
- Look over the characteristics of the events and determine how you want to analyze them
- Set your event sampling for the level you find useful and efficient for this stage in the process
- Test your search commands against the resulting subset of data
- Keep going through this process until you have a search that you are happy with

When you are done, make sure to reset event sampling to **No Event Sampling** before saving your search query to a dashboard, otherwise the previous setting will be included in the dashboard panel and will indicate results that do not show a complete picture of the entire dataset.

Splunk Universal Forwarders

Although detailed descriptions of Splunk Universal Forwarders will not be part of this book, it is good to mention that on large-scale Splunk implementations, data gathering should, as much as possible, be done using these. Their usefulness lies in the fact that they are lightweight applications that can run on many different operating systems and can quickly and easily forward data to the Splunk indexer.

Throughout this book, we have indexed files locally on your machine. In production environments, with many different types of deployment and using many different machines, each machine where data resides will have a Universal Forwarder.

When the implementation is large and includes many different machines, Universal Forwarders can be managed using the forwarder manager.

These forwarders and the ability to manage them easily are one of the reasons for Splunk's growing popularity. Sizeable organizations find it much easier to be able to bring in, understand, and use their data for decision-making when they can use the capabilities of Splunk's Universal Forwarders. It is useful to note that the adjective Universal represents the fact that Splunk can be used with almost any type of data imaginable, thus multiplying the usefulness of these Universal Forwarders.

Advanced queries

There are various kinds of advanced query that you may want to consider as you plan out how you will create searches and dashboards for your data. Consider the ones that we present, for they will help you design queries that are more efficient and cost effective.

Subsearch

A **subsearch** is a search within a search. If your main search requires data as a result of another search, then you can use Splunk's subsearch capability to achieve it. Say you want to find statistics about the server that generates the most 500 errors. A 500 error is a general HTTP status code that means that something has gone wrong with the server, but it doesn't know specifically at this particular time what is wrong. Obviously, if you are responsible for running a website, you want to pay close attention to 500 errors and where they are coming from. You can achieve your goal of finding the culprit server with two searches.

The first search, shown next, will return the server address with the most 500 errors. Note you are setting the limit to 1 and giving the instructions (using the + sign) to just include the server_ip field:

```
SPL> index=main http_status_code=500 | top limit=1 server_ip
     | fields + server_ip
```

The result of this code is as follows:

```
10.2.1.34
```

In the second search, you can then filter your desired query with the server_ip value from the first result and ask for the top values of the http_uri and client_ip fields, as shown in the subsearch highlighted in the following code. In the subsearch, you are simply asking for the top http_uri and client_ip fields for data that has been piped through to that point, or the data from the indicated server with the top number of 500 codes. This information will be very useful to you as you try to pinpoint the exact problems with the web server.

In the second search, you can then filter your desired query with the server_ip value from the first result:

```
SPL> index=main server_ip=10.2.1.34 | top http_uri, client_ip
```

You can combine these two searches into one using a subsearch. Also note that a subsearch appears within brackets. It is important to understand that a subsearch is processed before the search is actually carried out or parsed:

```
SPL> index=main [ search index=main http_status_code=500
    | top limit=1 server_ip
    | fields + server_ip ] | top http_uri, client_ip
```

A subsearch can also be useful if you want to search on data that depends on what you have found in another dataset. For example, consider a case where you have two or more indexes for various application logs. You can set up a search of these logs that will let you know what shared field has a value that is not in another index. An example of how you can do this is shown here:

```
SPL> sourcetype=a_sourcetype NOT [search sourcetype=b_sourcetype
    | fields field_val]
```

The default number of results is set to 100. This is because a subsearch with a large number of results will tend to slow down on performance.

Using append

Once you have done a subsearch, you may want to add the results of that subsearch to another set of results. If that is the case, and you are using historical data, use the syntax provided here to append the subsearch:

```
SPL>  . . | append [subsearch]
```

You can also specify various timing options if you like.

Using join

You can also use the `join` command to join the results of the subsearch to your main search results, but you will likely often opt to use `append` instead, if you have historical data. Again, the basic syntax is simple:

```
SPL> . . | join [subsearch]
```

This will default to an inner join, which includes only events shared in common by the two searches. You can also specify an outer or left join. The outer join contains all the data, whereas the left join contains the data from events fulfilling the left search, as well as the events that are shared in common. You can also specify a field list for the join, instead of including all fields by default.

Using eval and if

If you need to create a field based on the data present in an event, you can use the `eval` command to create a field variable and use `if` to check for that condition.

The `if` function takes the form of:

```
SPL> | eval value=if(condition, field1, field2)
```

Say you want to create two additional fields during search time to determine whether a destination is in the East Coast or not. Using the code presented next, if a destination URI has NY, MIA, or MCO in it, a new field called `East` will be added to each of those events. Otherwise, Splunk will add a new field called `Others`. Once that has been done, this code will list the newly-created `Region` field and `http_uri` for all events, and will sort by `Region`:

```
SPL> index=main http_uri="/destination/*/details"
     | eval Region=if(match(http_uri, "NY|MIA|MCO"), "East", "Others")
     | top 0 Region, http_uri | sort Region
```

A little regular expression has been used here to do a case statement between the airport codes: `NY|MIA|MCO`. If the `http_uri` includes `NY`, `MIA`, or `MCO`, then its `Region` field value will be `East`; otherwise it will be `Others`.

This should now return the data with the new fields:

Region ⌄	http_uri ⌄
East	/destination/NY/details
East	/destination/MCO/details
East	/destination/MIA/details
Others	/destination/HOU/details
Others	/destination/WAS/details
Others	/destination/SEA/details
Others	/destination/PML/details
Others	/destination/AK/details
Others	/destination/LAX/details

20 Per Page ⌄   ✓Format ⌄   Preview ⌄

Using eval and match with a case function

You can optimize this query by using `match` instead of `if` and account for `West` and `Central`.

We also introduce the `case` function here. In the following illustration, you will see that we can set the value of a field by giving it a value of `Label1` if `Condition1` is `true`, `Label2` if `Condition2` is `true`, and so on:

```
SPL>    | eval Value=case(Condition1, "Label1", Condition2, "Label2",
          ConditionX, "LabelX")
```

Let us tweak the previous query to use `case` instead of `if`:

```
SPL> index=main http_uri="/destination/*/details"
     | eval Region=case(match(http_uri, "NY|MIA|MCO"),
       "East",  match(http_uri, "WAS|AK|LAX|PML"), "West",
       match(http_uri, "HOU"), "Central")
     | top 0 Region, http_uri | sort Region
```

The result will now properly classify the destinations based on the region:

Region ⬍	http_uri ⬍
Central	/destination/HOU/details
East	/destination/MCO/details
East	/destination/NY/details
East	/destination/MIA/details
West	/destination/WAS/details
West	/destination/LAX/details
West	/destination/PML/details
West	/destination/AK/details

How to improve logs

Throughout this book, we have seen examples of how logs can be used to make applications more effective. We have also talked about how logs can be used to troubleshoot problems. In this last section, we will discuss some basics, recommended by Splunk that should be considered when creating logs.

Including clear key-value pairs

It is important to remember that data should be structured using clear key-value pairs. Doing so will help Splunk carry out automatic field-extraction in the way it is intended to and will do so in a faster and more efficient manner. Remember that we are talking about one of the most useful features of Splunk!

A model for doing this is shown here:

```
key1=value1, key2=value2, . . . etc.
```

As you do this, remember that if it is important to include spaces in the values, in text fields, for example, you should surround the value with quotes:

```
key1="value1" or user="Matt Nguyen"
```

Although you may find this method is lengthier and more verbose, it conveys a real advantage when it comes to field extraction, as it will allow it to occur automatically.

Creating events that are understandable to human readers

If possible, you should avoid readers having to create lookups to understand the meaning in your data. One way to do this is to use tools that can easily convert binary data to ASCII or text data, and use the same format throughout the file. If, for some reason, you have to use different formats, simply create separate files.

Remember to use timestamps for all events

There are many reasons why you should use timestamps for all events. Above all, their use helps determine the sequence in which events occurred, so is invaluable for problem-solving, data analytics, and other uses.

Also remember the following:

- Include the timestamp at the beginning of each line, making it easier to find.
- Use four digits for the year, for readability and identification purposes.
- Be sure to include a time zone. Here it is best to include the standard GMT/UTC offset format.
- Measure time to the microsecond. This could be helpful for identification of sequences or problem-solving at some point.

Be sure your identifiers are unique

This is an obvious rule and is familiar to anyone who has used or studied transactional data, but nonetheless we include it here, just because it is so important.

Log using text format, not binary

It is very hard for Splunk to search binary data easily or meaningfully. Therefore, wherever possible, create logs that are in text format. If, for some reason, your data has to be in binary format, be sure and include metadata that is in text format, so that it can be easily searched.

Use formats that developers can use easily

It is important to consider the usefulness of your log format. When setting up logs, include formats that are easy for developers to understand. One especially useful format is **JavaScript Object Notation (JSON)**. **Extensible Markup Language** or XML can also be used, but JSON is somewhat cleaner to read.

Using the `spath` command, structured data can now be parsed in Splunk by many programming languages through the browser alone, without even using a server! Using the structured key-value pairs of JSON, you can easily use data with a built-in hierarchy, such as this email data, where recipient has a sub-level:

```
{ "sender" : "george" "recipient": { "firstname" : "michael", "firstname" :
"shannon", "firstname" : "chloe" } subject:"Building my logs" }
```

Log what you think might be useful at some point

As you look at your data, consider what you think might come in handy for answering business questions at some point. What would be useful for decision-making? What would be useful for problem-solving? What data might you want to use someday for a chart or graph? Be sure that you log in any information you think you might need in the future.

Create use categories with meaning

Be sure your categories convey meaning. Especially important are labels such as INFO, WARN, ERROR, and DEBUG, which clearly flag events that you want to pay attention to.

Include the source of the log event

Be sure to include information that conveys where the event came from, be it a file, a function, or a class.

Minimize the number of multi-line events

In general, it is good to minimize the number of events that include many lines. Sometimes, you will have to leave them as multi-line, but this can slow down indexing and search speeds. Other times, you may want to turn multi-line events into shorter events.

Summary

In this chapter, you have learned some best practices to employ when using Splunk. You were also shown complex queries that can further enhance your result set.

This brings our book to a close. We hope that you have enjoyed this adventure with Splunk. If have completed (or even mostly completed) the steps in this book, we can assure you that you should now have a strong knowledge of this important software. Splunk appears, as we write, to be growing more and more successful in the marketplace. It is positioned to become even more important as the **Internet of Things (IoT)** continues its growing influence on the daily lives of individuals and businesses. Splunk is a skill that will help you as you navigate the exciting world of data and all the advantages it will bring to our future.

Index

J

JavaScript logging
  HTTP Event Collector (HEC), using 201

L

latency 32
limited time frame
  searching within 208
logs, improving
  about 216
  clear key-value pairs, including 216
  developer- friendly formats, using 217
  events understandable to human readers,
    creating 216
  log event source, including 218
  multi-event count, minimizing 218
  timestamps, using for all events 216
  unique identifiers, checking 217
  use categories with meaning, creating 218
  useful logs, using 218
lookups
  used, for data enrichment 95

M

machine data 31
modes, searching
  fast mode 209
  smart mode 209
  verbose mode 209

N

Network Operations Centers (NOCs) 120
new fields
  extracting 42
Node Package Manager (npm) 167

O

oneshot indexing 206

P

panels
  Status Distribution visualization panel 130
  Status Types Over Time panel 131

visualizations, creating 128
PowerShell
  used, for testing HTTP Event Collector (HEC)
    195
practical applications, Splunk Development Kit
  (SDK)
  prerequisites 167
  saved search, creating 169

R

radio input
  creating 139
reports
  accelerating 110
  creating 101
rex command 58

S

Scalable Vector Graphics (SVG) 167
search commands
  chart 54
  eval 56
  rare 54
  rex 58
  stats 52
  timechart 55
  top 54
Search Processing Language (SPL) 13, 47, 61
search
  accelerating 110
  anatomy 48
  pipeline 48
  results, filtering 51
Single Page Application (SPA) 188
source types 39
Splunk app
  creating 14, 15, 17
Splunk CLI (command-line interface) 10
Splunk Development Kit (SDK)
  about 165
  practical applications 166
Splunk Enterprise
  about 7
  software download link 8
Splunk fields

Made in the USA
San Bernardino, CA
06 May 2017